FORGIVEN but
NEVER FORGOTTEN

"A *Story of Abuse Loss* & *New Life*

SONYA JOHNSON

Published by Lee's Press and Publishing Company
www.LeesPress.net

Editing by: Alison Kellom

Book Cover Design by: William Lee, Jr.

ISBN-13: 978-0997862348 *Paperback*
ISBN-10: 0997862343

TABLE OF CONTENTS

DEDICATION

This book is dedicated to my angel in heaven, Anthony Isaiah Johnson. The short time you were with me I will never forget. I think of you daily and the last time we played together. Mommy misses you so much. I love you!!!! Also, my children I have lost to miscarriages, I know you are in heaven with Anthony, looking down at me. Even though I never got the chance to see you, I know when I reach those gates in Heaven, you all will be waiting with your brother.

ACKNOWLEDGEMENTS

To my Parents Edward and Mildred Johnson, whom have supported me in everything I did. They never told me what I could not do and encouraged me to always do more. They were by my side for the birth of my first child and been there for each of my kids. They have never wanted anything more than to have all their children exceed in everything they do. They have always shown me that things will not always be perfect, and that's OK. It's how you handle yourself in those imperfect times. I love you both to the moon and back.

My first-born son, Davon, I love you so much. From the moment I set my eyes on you I knew you were going to be special. Having a child as a teenager was not easy. I was young and had to learn how to be a mother. We really grew up together, and I would not have changed it for the world. I am so proud of the man you have become and look forward to the future. Remember what I always say, "You can do anything you want, once you set your mind to it."

To my loving, committed and strong Husband, I love you so much. I came with a lot of baggage and you welcomed me with opened arms. You showed me how to love once again, even with my flaws. I thank you for always believing in me and being my #1 supporter.

At the time when I wasn't looking for a relationship, God sent you. In you, he sent me everything I ever wanted and much more. I thank you for being the best father to all our kids (Davon, Anna, Alisa, Alexis and Carlos) and for your unfailing love for our family.

To all my amazing, beautiful children. You all have a piece of my heart in so many ways. I love you all with all my heart. Never, ever give up on your dreams!!!

To my siblings Toshia, Ebony, Darnell, Damita and Marfie. Thanks for being there whenever I needed you. For being the support I needed when Anthony passed, I love you all so much.

To my Pastors John and Kaiya Butcher, thanks for opening your hearts and church to me and my family. Kaiya, thanks for listening to my story and encouraging me to write this book.

To my Uncle/Aunt, Pastor Victor and Katherine Johnson, thanks for all the support and ministering after Anthony's death. I love you both.

My publisher Lee's Press and staff, thank you for an awesome job and support with this book.

Gloria, owner of A Little Insight Photography, thank you for taking me out of my shell and producing wonderful pictures. It was hard for me to get out my shell, thanks for walking me through it.

To all my family, friends, supporters. There are so many of you, I don't know where to begin. Thank you all for the prayers, encouragement and support. Always giving your opinion at times, even when I didn't want it, but really needed it. I truly believe some people come into your life for a season and a reason. I have learned different things from all of you. I love you all!!

FORGIVEN BUT NEVER FORGOTTEN

"Shhhhhhh." That's what he said as he slid on top of her. He would kiss her on the cheek, and then grind on her with his clothes on until he felt relief. The smell of his breath made her stomach turn. It smelled like old cigarettes mixed with liquor. He had red eyes, those of the devil, and always had a smirk on his face when he saw her. He was a family friend, who would believe her? Her father would be in jail if he found out because he would have killed him without a second thought for hurting his baby girl. This happened to her at least once a week. He said it wasn't sex because he didn't take her clothes off. That was a lie. Renee would close her eyes and sometimes look towards the ceiling. Just thinking, if there is a God why is this happening to me? When he was finished, he would kiss her forehead and walk back to the living room, watching TV like nothing happened. This would go on and off for her first year of school, then it never happened again. Renee wanted badly to tell her mom and dad, but she didn't. He was very good at making sure she stayed quiet, and she did.

Chapter 1
TO BE A KID AGAIN

Renee was born in Gettysburg, PA. A small town with a mostly white population, that is also known for the Battle of Gettysburg. At that time, there was a hand full of black families. Everyone knew everyone. And everyone knew everyone's business.

Gettysburg was fun though. When school was out, Tot Lot was the place to be. Most of the black kids would be there, hell they practically all grew up at Tot Lot. It was a summer program for kids that was free. The parents could send them to a place that was safe and kept the kids busy. They would go on swimming trips, field trips to the local museums, you name it. Renee had cousins and friends that all attended Tot Lot, it was what they all waited for at the end of the school year. There was nothing like it! Those were the good ole days!

Renee was born to two loving parents, whom she never had to want anything from. They weren't rich, but they were not poor either. They were a middle-class family. Her father was a truck driver and loved race cars. His name was Raymond. He was 6'4" and all muscle. His family moved to the area when he was a senior from Jasper, FL.

Raymond knew what it was like to be poor and to live in the south. He had two daughters from two previous relationships. One lived in the next town, and the other lived in California. His mother and father worked at a fruit factory at the time. Raymond also had a younger brother who was the local minister in town.

Renee's mother's name was Ann, she was light-skinned, 5'6", and beautiful. She moved from Greenville, MS, to Gettysburg after she graduated high school. She was one of eighteen children, raised in the Deep South, where hangings and daily beatings of blacks was nothing out the ordinary. She moved to Gettysburg with her daughter who was three at the time from a previous relationship. Ann worked for a local book company and took classes part time at night. She was strict. she made sure Renee and her sister Taylor were always dressed good and looking their best. She didn't play when it came to discipline and neither did Raymond. If you talked back or did something wrong, you would get your tail tore up, and Renee and Taylor had their share of whooping's.

Raymond was always gone driving trucks, sometimes weeks at a time, while Ann worked long hours. Renee and her sister Taylor were latch key kids. Latch key kids were kids who wore their house key around their neck at school.

They came home before their parents because their parents usually worked late. Renee and Taylor would walk to school together, and then come home together. They argued like normal sisters, at least every other day. Renee was always chasing Taylor with brooms, and anything she could find. Although Taylor would chase Renee back, she would duck and dodge anything being thrown at her because she didn't want to get her hair messed up.

They had chores daily, and those chores had better be done by the time Ann was home from work or they would have their tail whooped. Renee always got her chores done, and then ran outside to play with her cousins Sarah and Angie. Sarah and Angie lived next door. They were all around the same age, just two years apart. They played in the park daily, making play salads from grass, and burgers from tree leaves. In those days germs were not a thought. They even sat in the grass and would act like they were driving cars. They played in dirt daily, it was the norm. Red light, green light, was their favorite game. Renee would lose regularly, but talk her way out of the loss. They could go to the park, which was right behind their home. Their parents did not have to worry about them being kidnapped, it was safe. In these days, people in the neighborhood even left their windows and doors unlocked.

The best memory for them was peanut butter and jelly sandwiches!!

"Angie, look at Renee smashing her sandwich to make it bigger," said Sarah. "Renee, you're just greedy, just greedy," said Angie. They would burst into tears laughing so hard. Renee would always try to make more of everything. She would smash her sandwiches to make them look bigger, it was something they would crack up about daily. If they all had chips, she made sure she ate the last one in her bag. Food was her passion, she loved to eat and didn't gain a pound. She and Sarah had that in common, eat for days, but still skinny as a rail. They got made fun of at times for being skinny, but it really didn't bother them.

"The light just came on!" said Sarah. The light was the street light on the block. Renee and her cousins knew when that light came on it was time to go home. If not, they would hear their mothers yelling from the windows. "Get ya'll little asses in this house, you see that street light on!" If only they could stay kids forever!!

Since Renee was born, Sundays was church day. Ann dressed Renee and Taylor to the tee for church. They had the fluffy dresses, and the white shoes that clicked when you walked in them. Their faces would be greased up with Vaseline and hair laid to the side with never ending curls. They would have that one burnt area on their ear from where the hot comb had touched their skin.

Even though their uncle was a minister, they grew up at another church in town. Renee and Taylor sat in the pews and would be playing tic-tac-toe while the preacher was preaching. You better not act up, you would have an "Imma get your behind when you get home," look from Ann. Church was also a time for Renee to see other cousins and friends from school. Even though she attended church every Sunday, she never really **KNEW** God/Jesus. She just knew you prayed to God in your prayers. You went to Heaven if you're good and Hell if you're bad. And because of what happened to her when she was younger, she REALLY didn't want to get to know him. Renee would listen at times when the preacher preached, she always remembered one thing he said, but at that time she didn't understand. *"If you forgive others for the wrong they do to you, then God will also forgive your wrongs."* Forgive, Renee thought. She would go back to when she was molested. She was never going to forgive that man for what he had done to her. So how would God forgive her wrongs? She was a child, she had not done anything wrong. What did that preacher mean??? She would ask herself. At the age of 12, Renee became close friends with a neighbor named Sherry. She was 27 years old, and she had two sons and a boyfriend that lived with her. They always talked about hair styles.

Even though they were years apart in age, they had become close because Renee's parents had a son 10 years after she was born. He was now two, the same age as Sherry's son. So, they always took the kids to the park together, and they built a friendship from there. Renee would see her at least once or twice a week.

Knock, Knock, "Hey girl, how are you?" said Sherry as they made their way up her stairs. Renee followed her to the top of the stairs where her kitchen was. Her kids were taking a nap in the living room where her boyfriend was watching T.V. He was a white man, he looked older, but Renee wasn't sure of his age. She never much talked to him besides hi and bye. He was the father of her younger child, who was around nine months now. Sherry was a dark-skinned black woman, and beautiful. She had a good job, a car, and her own place. Renee always thought, this is going to be me when I grow up, independent! She looked up to Sherry, Sherry always gave her good advice. That day something was off with Sherry, Renee could sense it, but didn't know what it was. Sherry was always very talkative and always smiling. She had a smile that would brighten a room with her signature red lipstick.

"Hey, I am getting my hair done tomorrow!" said Renee.

Sherry was cooking and had her back turned to Renee.

"What are you getting done?" asked Sherry. "I don't know yet, I wanted to borrow one of your hair books so I can look through it."

Sherry turned around to get a spoon, while keeping her eye on her boyfriend.

"Go ahead, and get it, it's on the table over there," said Sherry.

Renee turned around and went to get the book, at the same time Sherry's boyfriend got up grabbed the keys and started to walk towards the downstairs door.

"Where are you going?" Sherry said. "I will be back, I'm going to the store," he said and walked down the stairs.

Sherry stared at him as he walked and shook her head. Renee made her way back to the table.

"Renee listen, if you ever have a baby by a man, make sure it's someone you really want to be with. Don't just have a baby to keep a man, and definitely don't stay with a man because you have a child by him. You can't trust everyone!" said Sherry.

Renee had no clue where this was coming from, but she listened.

"Don't take no crap from no man, you hear me!" said Sherry now looking directly into Renee's eyes.

Renee didn't know what to say, "Okay…..."

"I'm sorry Renee. I'm just going through some things. Just remember what I said ok!"

Renee agreed, and they started back to talking about school and the kids.

The next evening, Renee went over to Sherry's. She wanted to show Sherry her hair. As she knocked on the door, Sherry's boyfriend answered. "Hey, come in!" he said. Renee followed him upstairs, the house was different. It felt cold and just distant, it could not be explained. Renee didn't know what it was, but it was different. The living room was messier than usual, the kids sitting on the floor playing, but Sherry was not around.

"Where is Sherry?" said Renee.

"Oh, she went out, she should be back soon!" he said.

Renee started playing with the kids for a while. Then she got off the floor, and sat in the chair behind her which was facing Sherry's room. The door was open, but the room was dark. The only thing she could see was what looked like a brown comforter hanging from the bottom of the bed. She couldn't really see anything else above the bottom of the bed. As Renee was looking in the bedroom, Sherry's boyfriend had seen her, and he got up and closed the door. Renee then stood up and laid the book on the table.

"Well, I have to go. Tell her I came by, will you." she said.

"Okay I will," he said. Renee looked at him in the face on the way out. He was sweating and seemed anxious, it wasn't even hot. Renee thought it was weird, but walked on out of the house. Sherry's car was parked in the parking lot which was weird. They only had one car. Renee brushed it off and walked home.

Three weeks later, Sherry's body was found in the woods seven miles out of town wrapped in a brown comforter. Her boyfriend was charged with the murder, and was convicted. Renee had to testify at the trial, and it was an experience that stayed with her. She would always remember how she sat on the stand to tell about her last visit with Sherry. Sherry's picture laid on the witness stand in front of her. Renee would stare at the picture and try not to cry. Sherry was smiling like always with that trademark red lipstick. Sherry had spoken to family the night before she went missing, but Renee was the last person who physically saw her. That next day that Renee returned to Sherry's house, Sherry's boyfriend had already committed the murder. Renee started to realize that's probably why he was so anxious, and the house felt different. Renee's conversation with Sherry would always follow her in years to come with her relationships. She never forgot Sherry, and thought of her often.

Dear Diary,

Today was hard. I found out one of my friends was murdered. Why do things like this happen to good people? She was so nice and a good mother. Why would this happen to her? What did she do? I know when people die, they go to heaven or hell. But why are they chosen to die? Who makes this decision? Will I die soon? I don't understand even more about this God. This God let me get hurt when I was young. Now he let my friend die. He is supposed to be this wonderful God, but he lets the worst things happen!

It was now that Renee started keeping a diary. She would talk about everything in it. She kept it with her daily. Her parents didn't even know of it. It was something that she held near to her. Her thoughts, and her questions. Even though her parents where there for her and answered any questions she had, there were still some things Renee would keep to herself. Through the years, Renee was relatively a good student. She never got in trouble and made good grades, until 8th grade. She was called a Nigger by a white girl at school. Renee was suspended for fighting. That was one name you were not going to call a black girl in Gettysburg, especially if you were white. Renee wasn't done there though.

She felt the girl she was in a fight with did not get the beating she deserved. Renee had plenty of friends. White, black, and Hispanic, it didn't matter to her. She felt everyone was considered her friend unless they crossed her, and you didn't want to cross Renee. Renee had a mean streak when it came to being lied to or double crossed by anyone. Her thinking was "You want to hurt me, I will hurt you 10 times worse!" That hurt usually came from Renee's mouth. She would cuss you out in the worse way, her words would hurt. Besides this altercation, Renee never really got into fist fights. She would use her mouth as backlash. Although she knew racism still existed, she never experienced it firsthand until now. Friday nights were big during football season in Gettysburg. Everybody who was anybody would be at them, from children to older adults. When she could attend again after her suspension, it was on. The entire school knew in advance that the fight was going down this Friday at the football game. Renee had made a wooden club in shop class, it was about 12 inches long, and her name was engraved on the side of it. She had already been tipped off that the other girl was going to bring a weapon, so she was going to be prepared.

The night of the football game she slid the club down her pants while getting dressed, so her parents could not see it. At that time, it was the Snoop Dog era.

Everyone, even the girls, were wearing baggy pants and big plaid shirts. Renee applied Vaseline lightly to her face and had her hair pulled up. She was prepared to use her club if she had too, and she did. When Renee and her friends go to the game, it was packed. They arrived "on the hill." The Hill was known for the fighting grounds for anyone who was going to fight. Since everyone basically in the entire middle school knew about it, people were already standing around waiting for Renee to arrive.

"I didn't call you a Nigger. I said you are acting like a Nigger!" yelled the white girl. "Bitch!" yelled Renee, and it was on from there. The next thing Renee saw were the paramedics transporting the girl to the local hospital, while she was being cuffed and hauled off to the local police station. She wasn't going to use the club until she saw brass knuckles on the girl's hands, then it was on. Renee was still angry while sitting in the back of the police car. How this girl thought either way of saying Nigger to a black girl would be OK, she didn't understand. She wasn't worried about her parents, she knew they would be on her side when it came to the N word.

Upon arriving at the jail, the cop released her cuffs, and told her to sit down until he called her parents. He then returned and had her club in his hands.

"It's not very lady like to walk around with a club, and you have your name engraved on it?" Renee was silent and just stared at him, she felt a knot on her head.

"You might have really hurt that young girl!" Still, no answer from Renee.

"You could be in some real trouble if anything happens to her," the cop just kept talking. Renee thought, would he be saying all this if she was the one in the hospital? Her parents entered the police station looking pissed. The police officer gave them the rundown of what happened. My dad finally spoke, "I understand everything that happened, but why you put cuffs on my daughter like she was a damn criminal?" he said. The police officer stated how it was standard procedure even if I was a minor. Her parents signed a release form, and they were on their way. The police officer kept the club Renee had, and stated it was evidence.

On the ride home, Renee told her parents exactly what had happened. One of Renee's friends had already told them some of the details when they called them.

"You know I'm not going to say anything about what you did but, you know you shouldn't have brought that club to the football game." Her father said. "And you had your name on it," her mom chimed in.

"Well, she had brass knuckles!" Renee said. "Well, I hope you have people that saw those brass knuckles because that will be self- defense," said her father.

She did. Weeks later the girl took Renee to court for her medical bills. She was not severely injured, but they claimed she suffered a small concussion. She also wanted money for pain and suffering. Renee knew it was coming, she was prepared with several witnesses that were at football game. This was one of the biggest fights of the year. Everyone was there to see it; her brass knuckles could be seen in plain view. They came to the game to fight, and they did. After the judge heard from all the witnesses the case was thrown out. That was the first and only time Renee ever had to fight in school and got in any trouble with the law.

Chapter 2
NOT A VIRGIN NO MORE

New Year's 1993, Renee is now in the middle of her freshman year in High School. Her mother and father were strong. Her mother and father were strong. Her parents adopted Renee's little cousin Elisa, who was four. Renee's brother was now six years old. Taylor graduated, and was living in another state attending college. Life had been great. They have moved to a new townhouse with more room. Renee just received her first car. It was a 1980 dodge, tan in color. It may not be the car she wanted, but it was a pair of wheels! She finally had some freedom. She could ride to McDonald's whenever she wanted and just sit in her car and eat. Or she could go for a ride through the battlefield and just think. Renee did that a lot, she thought of her life after she graduated. She didn't know where she was going to go to college. She wanted to be a nurse since elementary school. The one thing she knew for sure is that she was not going to be staying in Gettysburg.

Dear Diary, I got my first car today! I was so in shock. I am lucky, not all my friends are able to get a car because their parents can't afford it. I love my Parents, even though they are strict, I know they love me. Where am I going to go? I got WHEELS!!

"Girl we ready to ride now!" said Renee's cousin, Sarah. Sarah and her sister Angie had also moved not far from Renee, it was still in walking distance. Renee and Sarah were tight, they shared everything. They were two peas in a pod. "So, what's been going on with you Sarah?" "Nothing, same ole, same." Sarah had problems at home, and she felt like an outsider at times. Renee was always there for her to talk to. "Soon, we will be out on our own, living our lives as we want. A couple more years cousin, a couple more years!" "Until then, let's go to the mall!" said Sarah. They started to laugh and hopped in Renee's car.

That was her weekends, spending time with her cousin and friends, working and cruising. Renee was involved in basketball, track, and even taught pee-wee cheerleaders on the weekends during midget football season. She was tall and very thin. A size 0, and for the most part, a pretty girl. She didn't date much because she wasn't allowed, but had been sneaking talking to some guys here and there. Renee dated white guys, Hispanic guys, and black guys. She had been seeing someone secretly on and off since 7th grade, it was her "true love". His name was Ty. Ty and Renee knew each other since 3rd grade. The first time they realized they had a thing for each other was in 6th grade.

Ty was throwing a ball at recess, hit Renee's face by accident, and it was love at first sight. Funny, but true, that ball was the first real interaction they had with each other. Ty was tall like Renee, light-skinned and skinny. Renee loved his eyes. The way he would look at her during class breaks would make her melt. Her heart would beat fast when he was around. When he put his arms around her, she felt safe. All their friends knew they liked each other, but they never made it official. It wasn't that they were embarrassed or nothing of each other. What people didn't know is they spent a lot of time together. They would meet in the library, the park, and anywhere they could to be alone. They would secretly pass notes to each other throughout Junior/Senior high school. Renee would dream about Ty all the time. She would think about them being adults and married even. Renee would even sneak to his house weekly, when his mother was working, and they would make out in his room.

One evening Renee had told her Mom and Dad She needed to go to the library. Ty's house was on the way, where Renee was really going. "Ding Dong" "Hey, come in!" Ty said, as he turned around to run upstairs. Renee followed, and was led into his bedroom. Ty was so romantic, he had SWV playing in the background and candles burning. SWV was the group. They danced to the entire SWV tape.

9

Then their song came on, "I Get So Weak." They started slow dancing and kissing. Ty was a great kisser, he would always make Renee feel as though she was the only person in the world. He took his time with her, she never felt rushed to do more than she wanted to. "Do you want to do it?" whispered Ty. "Yes," whispered back Renee. That night, Renee lost her virginity to her first love. She didn't know how to feel, it was painful, but a good painful. It was Ty's first time too. They were two teenagers experiencing things they never have before. They might have been lost the first time, but they got better and better at it. The rest of the year, Renee would sneak to Ty's whenever she could, and every time that SWV tape would be playing. They would date other people, but somehow find their way back to each other.

It was summer of 1994, and R. Kelly was increasing the population through his sexual music. Hell, his songs were probably responsible for half of the '90s babies! O.J Simpson was being arrested for allegedly murdering his wife. So much was going on in the world.

The deal she had with her father was she pays the insurance for her car. To do that, she had to work, and she had no problem with that. Renee had just started a new job at a factory, working part time. The new job was boring. Basically, she was packaging boxes for a local distribution company.

She also worked at the local nursing home part time in the kitchen. She had been dating Mark. He was a white boy from Hanover, the next town over. They worked together at the nursing home. He was cool to hang with, but nothing serious. They could never go further.

His parents were racist, so she knew they never be together. They were young, why not have fun while you can, they thought. Renee's worst night was when she stayed out all night with Mark and some friends at a camp ground. It was her first real experience with liquor, weed, and cigarettes. They drank beer, danced to the singing group The Doors, and played cards all night. She had got so wasted. She felt free, she was smoking and drinking, this was a new experience for her. After about four drinks, the next thing Renee remembered was waking up 6 am the next morning in a camper with Mark.

"Oh, my God!" Renee screamed.

"What?" said Mark.

"It is 6 am, my parents are going to kill me!" Renee started kicking the empty beer cans and making her way out the door. Mark was still half asleep, looking around.

Renee and her friend got in her car, and took off. Her mind was wandering. On her way home, she passed her grandmother's house. She wanted to stop there, but then she thought it didn't matter where she went. When she got home it was going to be terrible.

9

As Renee dropped her friend off, her friend's sister informed her that both of their parents have been looking for them all night. Renee nodded her head and headed home. When she hit her parent's front door, her dad was waiting at the door.

"Renee where the hell you been all night!" yelled her mother.

"I got this!" said Raymond.

"Where you been?" he said.

"I was out with friends!" Renee said.

"We have been worried all night, calling all over the place and you just come in here like nothing's wrong!" said Raymond.

"Go get me a switch off that tree outside!" yelled Raymond. That was the worst whooping of her life. There was nothing she could do but take it. She had worried her parents all night long. Later that day, her father put a For Sale sign on her car. It was sold a week later. She didn't know at that time, but the fear her parents felt that night was nothing like the fear and pain she would feel in the years to come.

After that night, Renee didn't speak to Mark again. She blamed him for her staying out all night. He didn't put the drinks down her throat, but he didn't help the situation either. While working at the factory, Renee caught the eye of an older gentleman named Ryan. He was 10 years her senior. She knew him from around town but never spoke to him. What she knew was not good things about him.

That didn't mean too much to Renee, she always gave people the benefit of the doubt, until they showed her otherwise.

"Hey, you're Renee Jackson, right?" he said. "Yes, and you are?" "My name is Ryan; I know your family. I remember you when you were knee high, but look at you now." Renee began to blush as she watched Ryan look her up and down. He was older, not like the childish boys in school. He was known around town for selling and doing drugs and being a womanizer. He didn't look like he was a drug dealer or user to Renee. He was handsome, thick eyebrows, good teeth, and had money. Sparks flew, and from that day on, Ryan and Renee were inseparable. They would take long walks in the park, and just talk. Because of their age difference they decided to keep the relationship under wraps. Now Renee was 17 and Ryan was 27. No one knew of the relationship, but her cousins Sarah and Angie.

"You're dating who?" Sarah said. "I heard he was trouble, you know he's been to jail!" Renee was smitten by him. There was nothing anyone could say to make her feel different. She wanted someone that was mature.

"Girl, yes, I know he's been to jail! That's in the past. We plan on moving when I graduate and get a house," said Renee. It was true, she had barely known him for a couple weeks, but Ryan had brain washed Renee already.

26

9

Ryan had it all planned. They would move down south after Renee graduates and live with his brother until he could find work. Angie was in disbelief, she walked away she was so upset at Renee. "What about Ty, I thought you two were doing good?" said Sarah. "Ty is doing his own thing, he's changed." "We used to be close and sneak to see each other as much as possible; he's just not the same." Renee stated. Renee started seeing a change in Ty after they had sex a couple times. She just figured hey, he got a taste of what it's like and wants to venture out. She wasn't mad though, she was over it, and she wasn't going to stalk him. "You and Ty have been feeling each other since grade school. I just don't believe you guys are totally done," said Sarah. Sarah was right, it didn't matter how much Renee and Ty denied each other. They been on and off since 6th grade, they were now both seniors. "You just don't wake up one day and say, oh I have no feelings for that person anymore Renee!" Sarah said. Renee stared out over the picnic tables they were sitting at in the park. Ty and his boys just happened to be playing basketball at the time.

Deep down she did miss him, but she didn't want him to know that. Renee never showed her emotions, she always kept them bottled up.

As Renee looked out at Ty, she saw Ty staring at her from a distance. "Man, what are you doing?" One of Ty's friends yelled at him for missing a pass.

Ty looked back at his friends, "Sorry man, let's play," and he continued playing basketball. "

You're right Sarah, I didn't think we would ever grow apart, but it just happened that way." Renee said. "What can I do about it? He's moved on and so have I. I guess we're not kids anymore."

Sarah could tell by the tone in Renee's voice that something was still there with those two, but she wasn't going to interfere.

"Look cuz, I'll be here for all your decisions, but I just want you to be careful. Ryan is trouble. You might not see it now, but you will, and I don't want nothing to happen to you!" Sarah said. "And how old is he? Isn't that statutory rape?"

"Sarah, I think we're in love, it's like nothing matters when I am with him. He makes me feel so loved. He buys me anything I want. I just can't wait till we can be together all the time!" Renee said. She had a big smile on her face, and her eyes closed as she thought of the moments she shared with him.

"Yeah, but I bet you don't feel the same way about Ryan as you do Ty." Renee was silent. Sarah saw the look in Renee's face and hugged her. "I'm sorry, I just love you," said Sarah. "Be careful cousin, just be very careful!" Sarah was right. The summer of Senior year Renee found out she was pregnant. "What are you serious? Yes!" said Ryan. Renee had just told him the news.

"You're happy?" said Renee. "Babe this is what I always wanted. You, me, the baby, us!"

"Yes, but I am still in school, we don't have an apartment, and my PARENTS, OMG what am I going to do!!" Renee screamed.

"Babe I am here for you, we will do this together. I am going to pick up another job to support us." They began to kiss and hold each other. Little did Renee know this was the beginning of a nightmare.

Dear Diary,

I am having a baby!!! I always wanted a baby, when my mother first brought my brother home I was in awe. The smell, the tiny fingers one by one. But wait, my parents. What will they say? But I'm in love! I have an older guy who will take care of me. I don't have to worry about anything. My boobs are sore all the time. Is this normal? How big am I going to get? I should see how far along I am. Where can I go without my parents knowing?

Renee was three months pregnant now. She went to the local Planned Parenthood and got an exam. She went there because she was told they would not tell her parents, and they didn't. That was something she had to do herself, but she didn't know how. She used red gelatin in pads each month so her mother would not notice she did not have a period.

Renee didn't know how she was going to break the news to her parents. The only person who knew, at this time, was Ryan. She was starting to show. This secret would not be a secret for very much longer.

Dear Diary,

My belly is getting bigger; I don't know what to do! I am so afraid to tell my parents about the baby. My father was always there for me, and that's what I want my baby to have. But Sherry always told me don't stay with a man because you have a baby by him. I wish I would have asked her more questions. What if you really love the guy? I feel so alone right now, I love you my baby. That's all that matters.

Renee decided to call her step sister Desiree. Desiree was two years older than Renee, and lived in California. She knew if she told her she wouldn't say anything to anyone. They had a close bond like that, even though they were miles apart, they still were close. "Hello" Renee whispered. "Hello, what's up girl!" said Desiree. "Oh my God, I have to tell you something, you can't say anything!" Renee whispered while slightly shaking with excitement. "What girl, you pregnant?" Desiree said laughing. "How did you know?" Renee said shocked.

"Because I am pregnant too, I just found out!" Renee was in shock and happy at the same time. She suddenly felt relief, she was pregnant, but her sister was too. They were going to have babies around the same age. "I can't believe it. Have you told dad!" Renee said with excitement.

"NO, girl, not yet, I haven't even told my mom!" Desiree said.

"Well I have to say something. I'm starting to show. My plan is to tell Grandma then have her tell them with me," Renee said.

"When you tell him let me know then I will call and tell him about me." They both burst into laughter. The situation wasn't funny, but they had to laugh to keep from crying.

"Daddy can I spend the night at Grandma's?" Renee asked. "Go ahead," said Renee's father.

Renee was going to break the news to her grandmother. Grandma Mable always was easy to talk to, she was going to listen without judgment. Renee thought maybe if she tells her grandmother, it would be easier to break it to her parents. She couldn't do it.

All night at her Grandmothers, they watched TV and hung out. She couldn't bring herself to tell her, but her Grandmother knew something was up. Renee could tell, as they watched TV. Her Grandmother would look over at her from time to time and smile, with her cigarette in one hand, and her Budweiser in the other.

There wasn't too much that you could get over on Grandma Mable. Renee's heart was racing. In her head she thought, "Ok, just say it! I'm pregnant Grandma," but it wouldn't come out. That night when Renee went to bed, she cried to herself. She thought what is going to happen? How is she going to provide for this baby? Is Ryan going to help or is he going to be in jail?

The next day Renee's mother picked her up from her grandmothers. Renee was depressed. What was her next move? She couldn't keep this pregnancy hidden for too much longer. She could feel her belly getting bigger. The baggy clothes were not going to work too much longer. Renee was tall and skinny, anyone who knows her would be able to tell soon. This has gone on too long. Tonight, was going to be the night that Renee tells her parents.

"I have to talk to you guys." Renee said. Her voice was shaking, her knees were trembling, and she had an ache in her stomach.

"I hope it isn't what I think it is!" gasped her mother. "I'm pregnant," said Renee. "WHAT!" screamed her mother.

Renee's father was calm, surprising to Renee. She was more scared of what her father was going to say and do than her mother.

"Well, all I can say is you almost grown now, you make your bed, now you must lie in it," said Renee's father. That's it? Renee thought.

Well, he was right, it was her senior year, and she would be 18 in a couple of months. Renee's mother was of course flipping out. Renee had faded her out. She was feeling relief, it was out finally! Then she heard her mother say, "Abortion." In the heat of the moment, Renee yelled out. "No, I am not getting an abortion, and besides it's too late for that, I am four months! Ryan and I are going to get an apartment when I graduate and move!" Renee said.

"Ryan, Ryan who? I know you don't mean Ryan Smith?" screamed Renee's mom. "He uses drugs. Do you know he was in jail and has a girlfriend?"

"He is not on drugs mom, he used to be on them. He also does not have another girl besides me!"

"He is 10 years older than you, what were you thinking?" Renee's father said. "I'm going to whoop his ass when I see him!" Renee just remained quiet as she listened to her parents go back and forth on the situation. As she began to slowly walk away she thought, "They don't understand what me and Ryan have, they will see. We will be one happy family." Well, Renee's parents were right. Two months before her due date Renee found out the truth. The entire summer Ryan had been on work release during the days at work. He didn't take on another job at night like he was saying, he was going back to jail.

The women, well yes, there were lots of other women. While he was telling her he loved her, he was telling three other girls the same thing. As for drugs, he was using more than selling. He had been dealing crack cocaine as his choice of drug, and was now allegedly using. Renee and Ryan still were together in her eyes. Even though she knew the truth she still wanted her dream family that he had promised her.

Chapter 3

ON HER OWN

"Push Renee!" said Renee's mom. It was April 8, 1995 at 10:40 am. Ryan Ray Smith Jr. was born. Renee had gone into labor the night before. She had phoned Ryan to let him know that she was having contractions, but he did not come. Renee went through 10 hours of labor, with her parents by her side the entire time. She was exhausted, but Jr. was so beautiful. He was 6lbs 5ozs. He had a head full of hair, and was white as snow. Yes, white! If Renee hadn't seen him come out, she wouldn't have believed that was her baby.

The entire time she was giving birth, she thought of her grandmother by her side in spirit. Grandma Mable had passed away a couple months before from a stroke. She would never forget seeing her grandmother in the coffin. Renee's heart hurt so much from her grandmothers passing. She kept it bottled inside. There's not a day that passed that she didn't miss seeing her smile when she would look at Renee. The last thing she always remembered her grandmother saying was, "I sure hope I'm alive to see that baby born!" Then she would smile. She was there. Renee felt her spirit all around.

"You sure you ain't been with no one else?" Renee's dad asked, while laughing. "That baby look white, he ain't got no darkness around his fingers or nothing."

"NO dad, I haven't, its Ryan's!" Renee said. In the back of her mind she wished she had been with someone else, specifically Ty. Ryan hadn't called or came to hospital yet. It was now 6 pm, no call, visit or anything. Renee had so much anger built up inside of her she could scream.

"Alright, were going home," said Renee's mom. "We will be back in the morning." Even though Ann wanted Renee to have an abortion, all that changed shortly after Renee's first sonogram. Ann couldn't wait till Jr. was born. She was the first person to hold Ryan when Renee had him, and she was immediately attached. As her parents walked out, Renee closed her eyes. She needed rest. She was sore in places she never been sore. Renee had an epidural early in labor, but it had worn off by the time Jr. was born. She felt it all. Just as she was closing her eyes, she heard a familiar voice.

"Hey sexy!" It was Ryan. Renee smiled as he leaned over and gave her a big hug.

"Where were you? How could you miss the birth of your only child!" She cried out.

"Baby, I'm sorry. I caught up in a fight and lost track of time. It's a long story." He explained. "Is that my baby? Can I hold him?"

As she handed over the baby to him, she noticed dried blood spots on his shirt. "Maybe he did get in a fight," she thought. He's here now, and that's what matters. As Renee watched Ryan with the baby, he was so gentle. "He's light, why is he so white?" Ryan said. "I don't know, he just is." Renee said.

Ryan stayed with Renee for the next couple hours. Talking and playing with their new baby boy. It was nice. Renee wondered, "This might work. We might be able to still be together." She thought.

"So where do we go from here?" Renee asked Ryan. Ryan sat back with his hands on his head and said "I still love you, I want us to be a family. I think I am going to move down south with my family for a while," said Ryan. Renee was lost, confused. "You said you think YOU'RE going to move?" Renee couldn't believe her ears. She's been by his side the entire time people talked bad about him. Now he was going to leave without her. "Renee, your young, you still have to finish school. Your parents are not going to let you leave with me." said Ryan. "I'm 18! I can make my own decisions!" said Renee. She knew it was true though. Her parents were not letting her take a baby out of the state, especially with Ryan. Renee needed help. She was a teen mom with no experience. Now she was going to be a single mom with no help from the daddy.

"I will be back. I just need to get my life together. I have a baby boy now, my only baby boy," said Ryan. "Once I get a job and get on my feet, I will come back. By that time, you will have graduated and we can move together."

Renee sat back and looked up at the ceiling. She was thinking about her next step, school then what? She had a baby to think about now, not just herself. She could see Ryan with them. She knew that was best to have Jr. with his dad. "Ok, but how will you see Jr.? What if I need diapers, wipes?" Renee said.

"I will be there for you, anything you need. I will send it to you. I love you." As Ryan and Renee embraced, Jr. started to cry. "Well, I guess someone is hungry," said Renee. They both started to laugh as Ryan went to pick up the baby. "I have a baby boy! I love you Renee, and thank you," said Ryan.

A few months had gone by since the birth of Jr. Ryan had moved down south to Atlanta, and Renee heard from him two times since he left. He gave her one box of diapers and one bag of wipes since the baby was born. It was over. Renee was now one month away from graduating and thinking about her future. She didn't know what to do next. She knew she loved nursing and caring for people. She also knew she wanted to get out on her own. Renee started to look up different programs that could help her.

She had the support, her mom and dad were great grandparents. If it wasn't for them, she didn't know how she and Jr. would have survived. She got WIC for the baby, it helped a lot. They provided baby formula, her parents did everything else: diapers, wipes, babysitting, even getting up for those late-night feedings.

Jr. cried daily, all day, and practically all night. He would be fed, dried, everything, and he would just scream. Renee's father had to sleep in his work truck sometimes at night just to get rest for work the next day. Renee's mother would come in Renee's room, and get the baby when she heard him crying. At first, Renee would just lie in the bed and let her. But then, Renee started to realize this was her responsibility, not her mothers. There was nothing wrong with her parents helping, but Renee needed to learn how to take care of Jr.

When her two weeks were up and she had to return to school, Renee took on complete responsibility. She would stay up sometimes all night with Jr., and get herself and him ready every morning for school. She would drop him off at the school daycare, then walk down the hill and attend classes. At lunch breaks, she would go feed Jr., spend some time with him, then return to school. She had a responsibility to Jr. to be the best mother she could.

She was a parent now, there wasn't any hanging out after school with friends. Renee saw for the first time who her true friends were. All the friends she had before the baby came slowly faded. She didn't get sad, she kept her head up and continued doing what she needed to.

Graduation day was here. Renee walked down to get her diploma and in the background, she heard Jr. crying. That's my baby, she thought, as she smiled towards her family holding up her diploma. It was a day of enjoyment, no more school. No teachers nagging about homework, no weekly test. Most of Renee's friends had picked their college and was ready to leave. The others stayed behind in Gettysburg, and started working and going to community college. There were programs for single mothers through the welfare system. Renee was encouraged by her social worker to take advantage while she could, and she did. She applied for housing, welfare, and food stamps. She already had the medical insurance. Renee knew she wasn't the type to be on public assistance, but she had to take care of her child. Two months later, Renee was living on her own. She was able get a two-bedroom apartment through housing. Housing rent is basically based on your income. She enrolled in a program that assisted her in professional development. She learned how to type and use different computer programs.

They gave her vouchers for clothes, bought her a car, and paid the first year of insurance. Renee was collecting welfare, something that she never thought she would have to do, but it was helping a lot.

Now, Ryan was back in Pennsylvania, but was sent up state for approximately two years for possession of drugs. Time was going so fast, and Jr. was growing every day. Renee was getting the hang of being a mother.

Everyday her mom would come on her lunch breaks to see the baby. She worked right across the street from Renee's apartment.

"Did you feed him yet?" Renee's mom asked. "Mom, are you serious, yes he ate, its noon time!" Renee said. Renee loved her mom, but the daily lunch visits were wearing her down. Ann would come over at lunch, and then again after she got off work. "I'm just asking, he acting like he's hungry!" Ann raised her voice. That was Renee and Ann's usual time spent together. Ann asking Renee did she do this or that with the baby. "Mom, I know how to take care of my baby!" Renee would say. Then Ann would usually repeat. "Well, nobody knows everything, I was just asking!" Renee rolled her eyes. She knew her mom meant well, so she bit her tongue and listened.1995 was coming to an end. The New Year was slowing approaching. Renee kept herself busy with her study program and Jr. She was dating again, his name was Josh.

He was a white guy, he was sweet. She started dating Josh a couple months after Jr. was born. He treated Jr. as his own. He bought diapers, gifts, and did more than Jr.'s real father because he wasn't around. It wasn't a serious relationship. Even though Josh's mom was ok with him dating Renee, his dad was not. He didn't like black people, and he made that known. When Josh would stop by his parent's house to get something Renee would stay in the car.

"You better not bring that Nigga in this house!" That's what Josh's dad would say to him when he would run in. He would tell Renee everything his father would say. Renee did not show emotions. She knew it would never work, but she wanted someone to be with. Even though it was 1995, racism was still very much alive, and especially in Gettysburg. Renee didn't care about skin color, if the guy treated her right and accepted her son, she didn't have a problem. Renee and Josh dated for a little over a year, then they called it quits. Josh was in love. He didn't want to be without Renee. "What did I do, I thought you loved me?" said Josh. "I do, but me and you both know it's never going to work. Your father would never accept me, never less my child, and that's a problem." Renee stated. Josh knew the truth, and he didn't care, he still wanted his readymade family. "I have bonded with Jr. I think of him as my own." Josh said.

"I know you have, and that's why it's so hard." she said. Jr. had bonded with him, but she knew if she didn't end this now, it would be harder later. Josh, wouldn't let go though, he came by daily after they split. He believed if he stayed around and spent enough time with Renee she would change her mind. This went on for a while, and then it slowly stopped.

When that stopped, Ty was there waiting to come back in. Renee never said no, she knew what the relationship was with him. Remember, they have known each other since grade school, when one said something the other would finish. They would spend time together mostly when Jr. was at her parents. She didn't want Jr. seeing another man, when she knew they were not an item. Ty and Renee had long nights to themselves drinking and making love. He still lived with his mother, so being able to stay at Renee's was the life. It wasn't like when they had to sneak around in their younger days. They could run around butt naked in her house and no one could see, and they did. The life, she thought I can do what I want, when I want, and not have to answer to no one. Life was good, and it was just the beginning!!

Renee was at home one afternoon and heard the doorbell ring. "Who is it?" she screamed. She was just about to feed Jr. "It's Ryan!" What! Renee ran into the bathroom to check herself out in the mirror.

"What the hell is he doing here!" she thought as she combed her hair. "Hey, are you going to open the door or what?" he screamed from the other side. Renee rushed to the door and opened it. It was him, in the flesh. Her heart fluttered. He still looked the same, he had gained weight, but it looked good on him. "Well, you going to let me in?" Ryan asked as he stared into her eyes. Renee stood back, and let him through. Once in, Ryan grabbed her by the waist and they starting to kiss. It was a long kiss. She hadn't seen Ryan since the day after she left the hospital. It was like he never had left, his kiss still made her weak for him.

"Where's my son?" Ryan asked as he let go of Renee. Jr. was in his high chair staring at them. "There he is! My boy, hey man I'm your daddy." Ryan began to pick him up. Jr. belted out a big cry. "What is wrong with him?" Ryan asked Renee. "He doesn't know you!" "Well, whose fault is that? You never brought him to see me," Ryan said. Renee put Jr. back in his high chair. She twisted her head around with quickness. "Have you lost your mind? You have been in jail since he was born!" "You left me with a baby all by myself!" She started to raise her voice and Ryan raised his voice. "You were not by yourself, you had your parents!" Renee became enraged. "Are you serious?! This is our child, not my parents, you and me are responsible for him!"

Ryan ignored her and started playing with Jr. "Ah, hello, are you listening to me? "she said, while turning him around.

"I hear you Renee, I'm sorry. I know I haven't been the greatest father to Jr. That's why I am here, to start to do the things I promised you."

Renee was still leery about Ryan, but he was here now, and he wanted to be with her and Jr. "Are you out of jail for good?"

"Well that's the thing, I was able to get moved back to the local jail here and get on work release." He said. "Wait, so you're supposed to be working now?" she asked.

"Yes, they let me out to find a job. I have to be back by 5pm." "It's all good though, I have a job already lined up." Renee was not impressed. He was out, but not really.

"I can start to help with Jr. We can be a family now." He said. "How do you figure that, Ryan? You're still in jail! I need to see a change before we can get back together." She said.

"I promise I will show you, you won't be sorry." Ryan grabbed Renee, and they started to kiss. She could not resist him, it was her baby's father. She was going to finally have her family complete. Even if her family did not care for Ryan, he was Jr's father, and they had to respect that.

Ryan started working. He would get off early at least two days a week and come to see Renee and Jr.

Most of the time Jr. was sleep, which gave Renee and Ryan time alone. That led to them having sex basically every time he came for a visit. Renee knew it wasn't going anywhere. She had heard from the streets that he was still out sleeping with other girls. That might be true, but she was the baby's mama, no one could ever come between that, so she thought. Besides, little did Ryan know, she was still talking to Ty between this time. Of course, they were not seeing each other as much, now that Ryan was coming by. But Ty was still in the picture. Ty wasn't crazy. He knew Renee's baby's daddy was going to be in the picture until Renee had had enough. Besides, Ty was out doing his thing too. He wasn't waiting around for her, at least that's what Renee thought. The visit, well, "booty calls," lasted for about four months. Then Ryan was caught at another girl's house when he was supposed to be working. He was taken off work release, and time was added to his sentence, and he was sent upstate again.

After that mess, Renee started dating other guys. She fell hard for a guy who was from Florida, but had moved to Gettysburg his last year of high school. His name was Nino. He was 6'2, coco complexion with gold teeth. He wasn't really Renee's type, but he knew how to smooth talk her. Nino sold drugs and Renee knew all about it. She would stay up late and count money with him if he needed.

Drugs never stayed in her home, they were always buried on the battlefields in Gettysburg. No one would look for anything there. Half of the people in town didn't even go to the battlefield at night because it was supposedly haunted. When Renee's parents took Jr. on the weekends, she and Nino would get high all-night smoking weed. They would never do anything besides weed. Renee and Nino had family members hooked on cocaine, and knew they would never try that. Selling cocaine was an entirely different story. They made a lot of money in Pennsylvania, and I mean a lot. He made sure she was always taken care of. Renee enjoyed the life at first, but then it got old. Smoking weed, and looking over her shoulder every day was not what she wanted. She wanted more in life, more for her son, and she was not going to find it in Gettysburg.

It was time for a change of scenery. Renee just finished the study program, and was now a Certified Nursing Assistant. Renee knew if she stayed in Gettysburg she would be stuck at a dead-end job, and probably have several kids. It was time to move on from Ryan for good and start a new life with Jr.

Chapter 4
SLIP UP

It was March 1997, on the eve of Renee's 20th birthday. She moved to Frederick, MD. It was about 30 minutes away from her home town of Gettysburg. She had a new truck and a nice two-bedroom apartment in the heart of the city. It was nice and roomy. Jr. had his own bathroom and so did Renee.

She worked day shift at a local nursing home as a C.N.A. She didn't really like where she worked, but it was a job. She had started to make new friends at work. One friend she became close with was Michelle. Michelle was also a mother. She had two kids and was married to an army man.

Fort Detrick was the base in Frederick for the military. Renee had never been around so many men, and men were very attracted to her. She would go to the store and have a phone number in her hand from someone she had just met. This was new to her. She was used to seeing more white people around.

Now that she was in a predominantly black town, she fit right in. She and Michelle shared everything, clothes, cars and their deepest secrets.

Dear Diary,

This is a big move for me. I now have a job, a new truck, and a very nice place. I hope to meet lots of new people, and make good money. I am no longer on welfare, but I still get food stamps. I need it right now. I have a good job, but I want better.

The money I saved from being with Nino, I paid for the deposit on this place, and I bought all new furniture. I wanted a new start to everything. I wish Jr.'s dad would help, but that's a lost cause. I don't regret my baby, but I wish he had a different father. It should have been Ty, but what can I do now, I can't change it. It is what it is, but my baby will always be mine, I love him so much.

As for a boyfriend, I am going to continue to play the field. I have been hurt too much in the past. When I get hurt, I think about my childhood and what happened to me. Maybe that's why I don't trust men fully? Or why I have all this built-up anger. I feel the anger boil in me when I think about the lies and cheating that my past boyfriends have done to me. I have decided to be like most men, have my cake and have a little extra on the side. Do what I want, when I want, and how I want.

Renee did her share of dating. She was now seeing a guy named Doug. Then other men, that were just acquaintances, here and there. She was still seeing Ty on and off too. He would come down every other weekend and spend time with her. They both were dating other people, but for some reason couldn't get enough of each other. That connection was still there between them, it would never leave.

"What are we doing?" Renee said to Ty. They had just finished making love, and were lying in the bed. "What you mean, were having fun like we always do," said Ty. "Yes, I know that, but is this how it's always going to be with us?" Renee said. It was true, Renee and Ty really liked each other. "It's like we start dating other people, then when it's over with them, something keeps bringing us back to each other, "said Renee. Ty was silent.

"Renee, I have to tell you something. I am going to be moving to go to school." Renee slowly got out of the bed. "When?" What could she say, he was going to better himself. "Next week. It's about 2 hours from here. I won't have a car, so I probably won't see you for a while." Renee's heart just sank. Ty was her first love, and she didn't know life without him completely. She wanted to tell him, that she was ready to try to make it work. But she couldn't. He was going to college. She couldn't interrupt that, no matter how bad she wanted to tell him please don't go.

"Why are you just now telling me this?" Renee said as she tied her robe. "I didn't know how to tell you." They began to hold each other. It felt like hours, they just laid there together.

They talked about their first kiss, their ups and downs, and where they were at now. Ty was the only man that Renee "trusted" besides her father. She could talk to him about anything, including other relationships. Renee was holding back. She was madly in love with Ty, but thought Ty didn't want to be tied down with Renee and a child. Ty thought that Renee didn't want to be tied down, she was enjoying being on her own. He knew about her relationship with Jr's dad and other men, and thought she just wanted to have fun and not be in a serious relationship.

He wanted to be a couple even though he was going to be away, he cared for her that much. He wanted to be that father figure to Jr., and possibly her husband in the future. Little did they both know at the time, they both wanted to be with each other, and were both afraid to tell each other the truth. It wouldn't be until decades later they would tell each other what they were feeling at that time. By then, it would be too late.

Weeks had passed, Ty was gone, but Renee still had Doug. Doug was a military man she met months before she moved to Maryland at a friend's party.

They were never exclusive, and they both had no problem with it. They had rules. As long as one didn't see the other with another person, they were fine with that. Renee wasn't stupid, by now she was 20 years old. She was in her prime. She had developed very well. Large breasts, plump booty, and still tall and slim. She had also grown her hair out to the middle of her back.

Doug was a very nice guy, but let's just put it this way, he was not experienced at all. Sex with Doug was like having sex with a stiff board that only moved one way, but 10 times worse. It was like her first time with Ty. They didn't know exactly what to do, but at least when they did it, they learned how to get better at it.

With Doug, it was like he still couldn't find where the penis was supposed to meet with the vagina. It was quick, boring, and exhausting. She had to fake an orgasm every single time, and he could never tell the difference. After he was done, he would be out of breath, and Renee would be relieved.

"Hey girl, what you doing?" Renee had just phoned Michelle.

"Nothing girl, trying to take care of these kids, as usual."

"I hear that, Jr. is with my parents for the weekend. I just came back from dinner with Doug." Renee said. "Oh, lord you mean 'can't get right!'" They both started cracking up.

"Girl why you still messing with him, that's too much faking. If he can't get it right by now, he never will!" said Michelle.

"HAHAH you got jokes, but I know. I don't know why I still deal with him, he's so freaking cute though!" said Renee.

"Girl looks aren't everything, you better be glad you got back up meat, that's probably why you're not frustrated yet." They laugh.

"Girl whatever, you want to go out tonight?" Renee asked. "Girl, I told you I got these kids, my husband won't be back till next week! "Michelle said.

"Oh, my bad, well maybe I will stop by, I'm gonna go out and get something to eat." She said. "Ok, I'll be here," said Michelle.

Renee was bored, the baby was gone for the weekend, and she was not interested in calling Doug for a late-night rendezvous. She pulled out her black book. Renee had been keeping this book since her move to Maryland. She was surrounding by so many beautiful men it was hard to keep track. She didn't have sex with all of them, she was too smart for that. Renee had certain men for different needs she needed to be met. Let's start with Doug. Well, we know he's not great in bed. Doug was the responsible one. He was the one that would never put her in danger. He made sure when they went out he took care of everything. He was a real gentleman, he just was terrible in the bed.

Then there was Mike. Mike was also a military man. He knew of Doug, but Doug of course, didn't know him. Mike was cool he was the party guy. He would take Renee out to parties and show her a good time. Even though she wasn't 21 yet her fake ID got her in everywhere.

Now Mike was a beast in the bed, and always wanted to stay at her house. Renee had strict rules, out before her child woke up. He didn't like to listen so she always had to sneak him out while Jr. was in the bathroom. It was too much. Sometimes he talked about moving in. That was not what Renee wanted from no one at this time.

Evan, Evan was someone new. Renee just met him a couple weeks ago, at the hair salon. He was 40 years old, and part owner of the salon. They were cool, just good friends. There was no sex, just conversation. He was someone Renee would call on nights that she just wanted to chill and talk.

She decided tonight was a good night. She didn't want to go out, she just wanted to stay home.

"Hey, what's up?" she said while holding the phone on her chin.

"Hey Renee, what you doing?" said Evan. "Nothing, bored, just thought I would call and see what you were up to." said Renee.

"Wow! So, I'm the guy you call when you're bored? "Evan laughed.

"It's ok, sometimes you just need that one person you can call on anytime, and I am that person." They talked up till midnight, said their good-byes, and then Renee went to bed.

Renee woke up the next morning feeling nauseated and having extreme heart burn. What in the world is going on with me, she thought? When she looked at herself in the mirror she noticed she looked very flushed. Her face was pale looking and her eyes were slightly swollen, the same look she had at the beginning of her pregnancy with Jr. "No, no!" she screamed.

Renee knew only one thing could make her feel like this. Pregnancy. She quickly got dressed and went to the corner store and got a pregnancy test. As she was driving back to her apartment, the only thing she could think about was, this can't be happening. She was always careful when having sex, but there was one-time last month when her and Doug were having sex and the condom broke. They didn't think much of it because it was a small little area that split. There's no way anything came through there she thought, or could it?

Renee always practiced safe sex, since the birth of Jr. Although she was on and off with Ty, for the longest, they even used condoms.

Now, even though Renee was a C.N.A, she didn't really know a lot about the medical field. She was young, she knew how you got pregnant.

But she didn't know that just the smallest amount of sperm could make you pregnant.

What was she going to do? She didn't like Doug like that to have a baby, but if it's positive she's stuck with him for the rest of her life. The test says, positive.

"Doug, I'm pregnant!" she said.

Doug just looked into his lap, no words at all. It was complete silence. Renee gave Doug the stare down,

"Hello, did you hear what I said!" she raised her voice.

"Yes, I heard you, I just don't know what to say. I never thought this would happen," Doug said. "I mean is it mine? I only say that because we are in an open relationship," he said.

"Yes, it's yours Doug!" If there was a possibility of anyone else, you know I would tell you," she said. It was true, Renee might get her groove on, but she was always safe and careful. She was not the type of girl to put a baby on a man because of what he can do for her. She has one child already and taking care of him with no support from the father.

"So, what do you want to do?" she said. "I am not ready for a baby right now," he said. Renee was in shock, she never thought he would say that. She was thinking yeah, he will be shocked, but this. "So, what are you trying to say? You want me to have an abortion?"

The room was silent, neither of them said a word. "You know what, I need some time to think about this. "Doug began to get up and walk to the door, Renee followed. As they got to the door, Doug gave her a hug bye and then he left.

Renee was not having an abortion. She did not believe in it at all. She thought, if I must raise another child alone I will. But, she knew if she kept this child Doug would be there. He wasn't the type to just leave his child and not help raise him/her. That's one thing she knew for sure, he was raised to take care of his own.

The next morning while Renee was dropping off Jr. at the daycare, she started to have cramps in her lower stomach. She had them before, but this time it was sharper. As she got back in the car and kissed Jr. goodbye, the pain began to get worse. She phoned her job, and made her way to the hospital. Upon arrival, the pain began to be more intense. She then phoned Doug and said he would meet her there. Renee was hooked up to IV, had numerous blood tests, and a sonogram. For the first time, she and Doug saw their baby. It was basically a black circle, but it definitely confirmed she was pregnant.

"You are five weeks pregnant, per the blood test and sonogram," said the doctor. Then what is causing the pain, she thought? "You have a cyst on your right ovary that looked like it ruptured, it has not caused harm to the baby at all," he said.

Renee gave a sigh of relief. She looked over at Doug and he looked stressed. No expression at all, just kind of confused, and a "what have I got myself into" look.

"You are free to go, just rest and take Tylenol for any discomfort, come back if the pain persists." The doctor then turned around and left. Renee got dressed, and Doug followed her home. Once they arrived at her place, Doug looked like he wanted to say something, but couldn't.

"What's going on? You haven't said anything since we left the hospital," she said. "I don't think I am ready for a baby. I know it's your body and choice, but I don't think we should have this baby," he said. Renee just stared at him. She didn't know what to say. She knew he wasn't excited but thought eventually he would get over it.

"I really don't know what to say to you, I never thought you would say that to me," Renee said. They both just stared at each other. "I can't have an abortion. I could never see myself do that." She said.

"Well, I never thought you would get pregnant either, I mean we are just kicking it," he said. "Yes, we are, but when you have sex, that's the chance you take," said Renee.

"I got to go back on Base. You need to think about what I said. Of course, I will help you take care of the baby, but this is not what I want at this time in my life." He left.

Renee was in shock and disappointed, she thought Doug would react totally different. Renee cried on and off for the next couple days. "What am I going to do?" she thought. She called Michelle. Who else could she talk to about this besides her?

"Girl, you know I would say keep it but, maybe you need to go see Ms. Dee," said Michelle. Ms. Dee was a local psychic. She was good, she was never wrong, so people say. "The question is, what do you want to do? Yes, you would be a single parent again, but you would at least have support," said Michelle.

Renee had enough of that. She had been raising Jr. alone since he was born. No child support, or anything, and it was hard. Just imagine two kids. Yes, the child would definitely have child support and all because Doug was in the military, but Michelle was right, she would still be doing it mostly as a single parent.

"I think I will go see Ms. Dee. Can you make me an appointment for this weekend?" Renee said.

"Yes, I will call you back with the details," said Michelle.

Michelle had made an appointment for this Saturday coming up. Renee phoned her parents to see if they could watch Jr. They said yes. She told her mother she was pregnant while on the phone.

"You're what?" said her mom. "I'm just in shock. Well, you're grown. If that's what you want to do, there's nothing I can say. That's your life. Me and your dad will still be here for you, you know that," she said.

Renee did know that. Her parents were her number one supporters. She always was thankful for that, even if her and her mom did not always see eye to eye. She knew that if she ever called them for anything they would be right there, but besides babysitting here and there, she didn't. Renee felt that she decided to have a child young, and it was her responsibility alone to take care of that child and raise him. At this time, she was working a job, but barely getting by. She would never ask her parents for anything, it just wasn't their responsibility, she thought. Just then her phone rang. She looked at the caller ID, and it was Ty's number. She hadn't spoken to Ty since he left for college. As much as she wanted to answer the phone, she couldn't. She was now going to have another baby, she was not about to tell Ty that.

Saturday was here, Renee drove alone to Ms. Dee's. Wanting to turn around the entire time, she didn't want to hear nothing bad. But she needed some guidance, and this was it, at least to her it was.

"The way I do this is, I don't want you to say anything but answer yes or no," said Ms. Dee. Renee nodded her head stating she understood.

Ms. Dee started out talking about Renee's life early as a child, and she was right on. She spoke of her being molested as a child and how she felt. Then, she spoke about her parents on how they love her and want the best for her. Then it came.

"I see you are with child," then she stopped. She started to look really confused and stared into Renee's eyes. "Why do you want to have this baby? The guy will help support the baby, but he will not be your husband, nor will he be around like you would like." Renee was silent, and then tears began to run down her face.

"I don't mean to make you upset but, I am telling you what I see. You are struggling now with one child, it's not going to get easier." She then began to tell Renee about the challenges she would have if she kept the baby. "I am not going to tell you what to do, I just see what's in your future."

Renee thanked her and left. The entire ride home the only words she kept hearing was "Why do you want to have this baby?" I can't do this alone again, she thought.

When Renee got home she phoned Doug. "Doug, find a place and I will go get an abortion, but it needs to be done this week as soon as possible." Renee said. Doug sighed and stated, "Are you sure? I don't want to pressure you to do something you don't want to Renee, it's your body." "I am sure just find a place," Renee hung up the phone without even saying goodbye.

Dear Diary,

I have decided to have an abortion. I can't believe I am saying this. Not only because of what the psychic said, but because I don't want another child to come in this world without a father. I can't do that to another child of mine.

Children should be raised with both parents. How will they do this? Will I be in pain? I don't know. There are so many questions. I feel sick to my stomach. I have to make this choice. I don't want to have no more kids without being in a committed relationship or married, and I don't want to be married now with no one.

Chapter 5
THE ABORTION

A week later, Doug drove Renee two hours away to a clinic in Virginia. Upon arrival, they were both counseled on what was about to happen. The entire time the counselor was talking, Renee was mentally not there. In her mind, she was hearing. "This is the best choice, why do you want to be a single mom again? He won't be there like you want him to be, you don't want a baby by him, and you don't even love him."

"I am so sorry, but can we just get this over with" Renee said. The room was silent. Doug looked at Renee with his eyes wide open. He never seen Renee this way. He knew this had to be hard on her but he didn't know what to say. He just kept quiet, and looked at the counselor. "I understand. I will get you back to the room as soon as possible," the counselor said. A couple minutes later Renee was walked back to the room, and Doug was told to stay in waiting room. As Renee lay in the bed with her legs stretched opened, she stared at the ceiling. She grew up in the church, but never really prayed to God or spoke to him. But today, she looked up and thought about Jesus, nothing specific, just Jesus came to her mind.

As the doctor explained the procedure, Renee was still present but mentally in another world. The more he spoke the more she just heard...... "You can't handle another child, diapers, and late nights." Then in the blink of an eye, Renee felt extreme pain in her vagina. "NOOOOOO! "she yelled out. It was the worst pain she ever felt, like a knife stabbing her in her womb. "I can't do this awake!" she yelled. "Ok, Renee calm down let me get your boyfriend." The doctor stated. "He's not my boyfriend!" said Renee As the doctor went out to get Doug, Renee knew she could not bear this pain while awake. The doctor returned with Doug. "She has to be put to sleep, she is not going to be able to do this awake" stated the doctor. "How much is that going to cost?" said Doug. "Another $200.00," the doctor said. "I will have to go to the bank," Doug turned to Renee, "I will be back, just relax." Relax, Renee thought, did he just say relax? His legs weren't pulled up and stretched for the entire world to see. He didn't feel what she had just felt. Renee laid back and continued to look up at the ceiling. She thought about her past, being molested, Sherry's death, and Jr's father. Why did God let her get pregnant knowing this was going to happen? She was angry about it all, but didn't say a word. A tear began to flow down her face. About 20 minutes later, Doug was back. Renee was given medication through an IV.

Minutes later she was falling to sleep. The last thing she remembered was seeing the nurse standing beside her, holding her hand, and the doctor down between her legs waiting on her to fall asleep.

When Renee opened her eyes, she was in the same room. Doug was sitting beside her, and the nurse was doing her vitals. She felt empty. She was drowsy, and confused. She knew what had happened, but because of the sleeping meds her head was foggy. The nurse gave instructions for what to do when she gets home. Doug took the instructions, and guided Renee to his car. The entire ride back to Frederick, neither of them said a word. They didn't even look at each other.

Renee was done. She didn't want to have nothing to do with him anymore. He was cold, even if he didn't know what to say, he could have made small talk or asked her how she felt.

When they arrived at Renee's apartment, Doug asked her if she was hungry and made her some soup. He left a couple minutes later, and Renee was relieved. There was nothing else for them to say to each other. The damage was done, the baby was gone, and he was not going to have to be responsible for a child he didn't want. Renee didn't know at that time, but that decision she made would haunt her in the years coming. That day Doug walked out, was the last time she spoke to him.

Dear Diary,

I just now realized I killed my child!!!!! What have I done, will I go to hell? I am so confused! I think about this every night. The pain, I see darkness in my dreams. I see the doctor between my legs saying, "I t's complete," then the nurse walking away with a tiny baggy. I can't see clear what's in the bag, but I see something that resembles a small peanut that hasn't been cracked. Is that my child? Did I do that to my child? I'm I going to Hell! Can God forgive me? Is there forgiveness?

Chapter 6
THE BOUNCE BACK

It had been a couple months since the abortion. Renee was back to work and getting back to herself. She thought of her baby daily, sometimes she didn't sleep at night thinking about it. She had been spending more time with Jr. and her family, and just trying to enjoy life. She had just spent Christmas at her parents and broke the news of the abortion to them. They supported her in her decision. They did not believe in abortion, but it was her life. They couldn't tell her what to do, they could only be there as they have always been. While there, her father pulled her aside to talk. Renee loved those talks with her dad. He didn't always say what she wanted to hear, but she knew he was always right.

"How are you?" her father said. "I'm alright," said Renee

"Now I don't know what happened between you and that boy, but you need to think about who you're with. I may not go to church, but I believe god does things for a reason." Her dad said. "I can't tell you, you shouldn't have had an abortion or you should have, that's something you have to live with. But I know, you need to start thinking about who you lay down with and what you want." Silence.

Renee knew he was right, she needed to slow down when it came to guys. She was dating several men here and there. She didn't want this to happen again, out of the couple of men she was seeing, she didn't really love none of them. They were just someone she could call to have a good time, eat, and maybe even have a night cap, if she wanted. She didn't know what she wanted. She knew she didn't want to be married, that's for sure. She was only 20, almost 21. She had enough sense to know that she was too young to be thinking about marriage.

"Daddy, I know what you're saying, but I just want to have fun. I don't want to be tied down to one person!"

"Renee, I am not telling you to be tied down, I'm telling you to slow down."

Renee knew her dad was speaking from his heart. Renee hugged her dad, and they talked some more before they went in to join the rest of the family.

Renee was back home from the holiday weekend when she received a call from Evan. Evan would always call to see how she was, especially after the abortion. She had broken off connection with Mike and Doug, and wasn't really going out anymore. Evan and Renee never had sex, it was all conversation. She confided in Evan a lot. He knew about the other guys, and what she was going through.

He was compassionate and never asked anything from her, but her to be herself.

"Hey what are you doing tomorrow? Its Monday, so I'm off, thought I could finally take you to get your windows tinted, "Evan said. "Are you serious? You know you don't have to get my windows tinted, you crazy!" said Renee.

"No serious, you said you've been wanting them like forever. Take it as my late Christmas present to you."

Renee agreed. The next day she had her truck tinted with black out tint all the way around. Evan took her out to lunch, and then they went back to her place. They talked about their jobs, family, and looked at T.V a little. Then Renee had to go pick up Jr. from daycare, so Evan made his way home. For the next few weeks Renee's schedule was work, and spending time at home with Jr. Money was tight, and her job didn't pay well. Yes, she had housing, but she had other little bills to pay too, like credit cards that she got at 18. She ran them up on unnecessary things like buying herself gold herring bone necklaces, clothes, and other things that she didn't need. The drug money from Nino was wasted on stupid things too. Now, Renee was wishing she saved more of the money Nino was giving her rather than spending it.

"I need to find a part time job," Renee said to Evan.

"What you need? You know I can help," Evan said. Renee knew Evan would give her anything she wanted. He was basically a 44- year-old sugar daddy in her eyes. She knew he was not the kind of man she wanted to be in a REAL relationship with. He was just someone to spend time with, get some free meals, and chill. She had taken money from him before, a few dollars here and there, and not to mention the tinted windows. They were now having sex, but not often. To Renee it was ok, not the best, but hey, it was enough to satisfy her at the time.

"No, you helped out enough. I just need something at least on the weekends when my parents can watch my son," Renee said.

"Well, have you ever stripped?" Evan asked. Strip?!, Renee thought. She was not pulling her clothes off in front of some old men for money.

"Hell no!" I am not getting naked for some old freaky men!" she said.

"Ok, for one they're not all old, two you don't have to get completely naked!"

"What do you mean?" she said. "Ok, I part own a strip club about 45 minutes from here. It's clean and professional. You don't have to get completely undressed. You can take your top off or leave it on, but you need to be wearing something very sexy," Evan said.

"Why haven't you ever told me about this before?" Renee asked.

"You never asked," said Evan. It's true she didn't, but who would ask a question like that?

"Look, you can earn extra money. If you don't like it, then you can stop anytime," he said.

Renee thought good money, don't have to get naked, and no one would know me!

"Ok, when can I start!" she said smiling.

Renee was about to be 21 in two days, and she was ready to live it up. She was finally going to be legal. That weekend, on her birthday, she went to a local club with Michelle and a couple other girls from the Sands Projects. Sands were housing development for low income housing. Most of Renee's coworkers lived there. Even though she was on housing, she was lucky. Her apartment was on the east side in a ritzy neighborhood, and at that time her credit was A plus. Shante was one of Renee's close friend that lived-in Sands.

She was a spitting image of Jada Pinkett-Smith, everyone called her young Jada. She was three years older than Renee with four kids. Renee didn't see her as much because for one she was working all the time, and two the Sands was on the opposite side of town. The three made their way into Uptown, the local club, and it was on. This was Renee's first time at Uptown. 21 never felt so good. She could drink what she wanted, and get into the club, legally!!!!! Soon as they hit the floor, the DJ was pumping out "Too Close" by Next.

It was the jam, and the men were definitely way too close. Renee wasn't much of a dancer, but she danced until her hair fell that night from sweating. All the worries about money and bills were gone away, at least for now. It was getting towards the end of the night, and "All my Life" was playing by KC and JoJo. Renee was dancing with some dude she had just met. Michelle was also on the dance floor. Her husband had come and surprised her, and Shante was wasted at the table. That was Shante, could never hold her liquor. As Renee said her good- byes, Michelle volunteered to take Shante home so Renee can go straight home. "Did you have a good time?" Michelle asked. "Yes girl, I had a ball, thanks girl!" Renee and Michelle hugged, and they got in their cars.

Renee was tired. She had never danced so hard in her life! She knew she needed a good bath and some sleep. She had to be at her parents tomorrow to pick up Jr. As she got out of her car she could see a silhouette of someone at her door. "Who in the world is that?" she said to herself. Just as she started to walk, she heard.

"Well damn, you must have had a good night, its damn near 3am! "It was Evan.

Renee was taken back. She thought why is he here at 3am? "What are you doing here?" Renee asked. Right then Evan handed her a dozen red roses. "Thanks, but why are you here so late?"

"Well, I came a couple hours ago, to surprise you and to my surprise you were gone. Where were you?" he asked.

"I went out for my birthday with some friends. Forget that, you been at my door for a couple hours?" she said.

"No, I left and came back a couple times. I was going to leave these at your door, but since you're here, can I come in?"

Renee was not comfortable with this, he never did this before. They were not a couple, so why was he acting like it? She let him in, and Evan stayed the night. She was drained from the club, but after a good shower and massage by Evan, she was ready to "entertain his old ass," as she put it.

The next morning Renee woke up before Evan. She rolled over and just stared at him. He was 23 years older than her. He stood 5' 8", about an inch shorter than Renee, but he was muscular. He looked like he had been lifting weights all his life. He wasn't a bad looking man, but Renee knew he wasn't anyone she would take home to her parents. This was his first time spending the night. It was not going to be a regular thing, she thought. "Hey, wake up! I have to get going to pick up my son!" Renee said. Evan slowly opened his eyes as Renee was getting dressed. Evan started to get dressed. "Hey, don't forget next weekend is your first night. Are you going to be ready?" he asked.

"Yah, you said I get paid, nightly, right?" Renee asked.

"What don't you understand? They give money to you as you dance. Damn really!" He raised his voice.

Renee looked over at him. "You don't have to get smart! I just asked a question, I never did this before."

"You know what, I'm sorry, you're right. Don't worry, I got you." He said. Evan gave Renee a hug and they went their separate ways.

That week seemed like the longest week in the world. While at work, Renee could only think of what it was going to be like this weekend at the strip club. Evan had prepared her by giving her a bootleg of the movie, "The Players Club." In his words, "Study her movements in this movie, you need to move like that." Renee was Diamond in her mind. She had a baby young, and was doing what she needed to do to support her child. She looked at that movie about 12 times that entire week, and then it was time to put her skills to work.

Renee had just dropped off her son, and was about 30 minutes away when her pager went off. Oh yeah, Evan had gotten her that too. "BEEP BEEP 2222!" 2222 was his code for hurry. Hurry she thought? Evan had given her specific instructions to be there at 10pm to help her get dressed.

Renee pressed on the gas and made her way via the directions he had given her. As she pulled up to the club, it was dark. The only light you could see was from the lights on the building, it read "The Blue Starlight Club." "What in the hell have I gotten myself into!" Renee said out loud. There wasn't even a parking lot. It was all dirt in the parking area, filled with old trucks and Cadillacs. Just like she thought, and probably full of old men.

Renee entered the building toting her black book bag with the clothes Evan had bought for her. They were all thongs, with matching bras. Some had diamonds on them with bright flashy colors. She didn't know which one to bring, so she brought them all. The place was surrounded in smoke, it was loud and you could barely see anything. There was a Hispanic girl on the pole dancing, and several men around her putting money in her G-string. There were all ethnicities of men; black, white, Asian, Hispanic, you name it.

"Hey, Renee over here!" it was Evan. He grabbed her hand as she came close, and directed her towards the back of the club. As they made their way through two double doors, they approached a very small room. It had three chairs and a long desk attached to the wall with mirrors. There were three other girls getting dressed at the time. Renee was the only black girl.

"I would like you all to meet Renee," said Evan. "Hi, my name is Kat!" said the first girl. She was very pale, with long blond hair, and way too much make up.

"My name is Shannon and this is Gigi!" "Hi!" Renee said while shaking. She was nervous. This was not her type of setting.
What was she doing here? She was better off picking up a regular part time job, but before she could even think about turning around, Evan grabbed her hand.

"Ok, I need you to get dressed. You're on in five minutes!" he said. "What? That soon, man can I get relaxed first?" said Renee.

"Hey, you said you needed the money, and this is how you can make it!" Evan said.

Renee started getting dressed, she went to the furthest corner she could. How in the world was she going to strip in front of a room of men, and can't undress in front of females? Renee finished getting dressed and had a shot of vodka. Gigi had given her a shot, "Hey, if this is your first time you're going to need it! Just think of all of them being naked when you get on the stage," she giggled and walked away.

"You're up Renee!" Evan yelled from outside the door. "Please welcome to the stage, DIAMOND!" the DJ yelled from the booth. Diamond, Renee thought, really? Evan was taking this Players Club too seriously. This was it, now or never!

She was wearing a red and black two piece. She wore red high heels, in which she never walked in, so she was wobbling the entire walk to the stage. As she stepped on the stage, Renee looked out into the audience. Everyone was quiet. It felt like time stood still for a moment. She couldn't tell if she was drunk or what. She felt mellow though, real relaxed, and like there was nobody there but her. The music started, it was some R. Kelly. She rolled her eyes, go figure she thought. She slowly removed her heels and, started the moves she learned while studying, "The Players Club." When the song was over Renee, looked down and saw what seemed like thousands of 10 and 20 dollar bills. She grabbed it all, and headed towards the back room. It was over! That's it? That's all she had to do, she didn't have to get undressed at all. Renee started counting her money, $450 in less than 10 minutes. That was just the beginning. Renee was set! She could pay extra bills, and still have money to do extra things with Jr.

Renee started being a regular. Every Saturday she would go to the club and work. If her parents couldn't watch Jr., he would go to her friend's house. She was now bringing close to $700 home every Saturday night dancing 2 sets for about 15 minutes each. Evan was still there every single time, like he said he would. Watching, making sure she was safe, and counting his money at the door.

They had become an item now. Everyone in the club knew she was Evan's girl. Evan had ways about him that Renee did not like. Sometimes when she was at work, he would pop-up on her. He said he was surprising her for lunch, but Renee would see him sitting in the parking lot some days. When she would ask him later what he did that day, he would never mention being at her job. There were also nights that Renee looked out the window, and she would see his car parked behind a tree outside her building. In the back of her mind something wasn't right about it, but she shrugged it off. She also noticed if she was even 5 minutes late from meeting him, he would become enraged, but later apologize for his behavior. Renee was heading to the dressing room on the way into the club one night when Evan stopped her at the door.

"Hey, tonight I want you to do a little more!" he said. "What do you mean a little more?" Renee asked

"You need to take your top off at least, these men ain't going to keep throwing you money out and you ain't showing nothing!" he said.

Renee was taken aback. Show more skin? He never said this before to her. He knew the only reason she was doing it was because she didn't have to take anything off.

"Oh, I'm not doing that Evan! You said I wouldn't have to get undressed. Besides, I'm making all I need!"

She began walking away. As she made it into the dressing room, it was empty. Evan had followed her inside.

As she turned around to lay her belongings down, Evan grabbed her arm and twisted it around her back. With his other hand, he slammed her face into the mirror. The mirror cracked in the middle. As Renee looked into the mirror she saw blood trailing down her head. Evan was twisting her arm so bad she could feel a burning sensation in her shoulder. The look on Evan's face was pure evil, his nostrils were flaring, and he was spitting as he spoke. "Listen, I don't ask you to do much! I am telling you what I need you to do, and I need you to take your clothes off!" Renee was in shock and scared. Evan never got physical with her at all. Was this a joke, she thought.

"Evan, are you for real? I am not taking my clothes off, that's it!" she screamed.

Evan then let go of her, turned her around, and put his hands around her neck. He was squeezing so tight that Renee started to gasp for air. "If you don't get on that stage and do what I told you to, I will bust every window out of that truck that I paid for! Don't make me do something to you that I will regret!" he screamed. Renee stood in silence, she could hardly breathe. What was she going to do? Was he really choking her? She needed her truck for work, how was she going to take her baby to school? What has she gotten herself into?

"Okay, okay, I will do it!" Her entire body was shaking. Evan let go of her. She couldn't believe this was happening. Evan had never made a threat to her, or made her feel scared. She knew she had to do this show, there was no way out. No back door to sneak out of, and the bathrooms were on the other side of the club. She started to clean herself up.

"You have five minutes to get your shit together, and you better put on a good show! You and Kat are the only two here tonight so you have to dance at least three times!" He turned and looked at Renee before walking out, "Stop shaking and clean yourself up, I wasn't going to hit you, but I will hurt you in other ways, believe that!" he slammed the door.

Renee sat in front of the mirror, and just looked at herself. She was so pretty, why is she doing this? She had paid the bills she needed to pay off. Her job wasn't the best, but she could waitress on the side to make extra money if she wanted. The question now is, how is she going to get out of this? Evan had become dangerous overnight. As she finished getting dressed, the only thing she was thinking about was getting this over with and going home. No amount of money is worth taking your clothes off and being in danger. She thought about Sherry too. She didn't know what Evan was capable of after this. And she wasn't going to find out!

It was now Renee started having trust issues even more when it came to men. Evan was such a good guy, and overnight he had become a different man. Renee returned home that night a wreck. She had made a little over $1200. She would give it all back if she could erase that night. She danced topless all three times. Even though she was not completely naked that was enough for her. The next question was, how is she going to keep Evan away? He knows where she lives and he knows where she works. She didn't know what to do. As she got in the shower, tears began to roll down her face. She cried. She felt dirty even though she didn't do anything sexual. Just having her top off made her feel dirty.

Minutes later, Evan came over and they had sex. It was rough, and Renee cried throughout it. Evan was too drunk to see her cry, and he probably wouldn't have cared anyway. For the next week Renee dodged all of Evans pages and calls. She would see his car parked outside some nights as he called her house phone. She wouldn't answer, and she would let the machine answer it.

Friday was here, and she knew he was going to just show up. He was like clockwork. He knew Fridays were Renee's day to be home for the weekend. Not this weekend Renee thought! As soon as Renee left work, she picked up Jr. and headed to Gettysburg for the weekend.

She packed their bags that morning, and had the landlord change the locks. Evan never had a key to Renee's place, but she didn't put anything by him at this point. He'd been in her home with her several times, and she had spare keys around. That night Renee received page, after page, after page, after page from Evan. She didn't have a cell phone. The pager was his only way to contact her, besides her home phone. She decided to check her home messages. Evan had left eight messages since that afternoon.

"This is Evan. Call me!"

"This is Evan. Call me Renee we need to talk!"

"You know who this is. I've called you several times. I will keep calling you until you answer!"

It kept going on and on. Each message he got madder and madder. Renee turned the pager off and went to bed. The weekend went by. Renee spent time with her family, and went to hang out with old high school friends and relatives. She was not ready to go back home, she was scared. She didn't know what she was going to do. She didn't believe that Evan would physically hurt her even more, but she didn't put nothing passed him because she seen how he could get.

Sunday evening had come, and it was time to head back home. She looked at her pager Evan had paged over 20 times, 911. Renee didn't want to get her father involved. That would have been really bad.

She only had one person she could turn to, to get rid of this man, her friend Jay. He was a good friend of Renee's she met at work. They were true friends, they never had sex or dated. They talked about work and family, and kept it 100. Jay was a big dude. He stood 6'3", and was stocky built. She knew if she needed protection, he would be there. Renee called Jay from her parents, and gave him the run down.

"Renee, are you crazy, I know this dude!" he said. "Well, I don't know him personally, but I know about him. First off, he is married. He probably said he's not going to hit you because he knows you would probably go to the police, and he would have to explain to his wife." Jay said.

"Married? He told me he was divorced years ago!"

"NO! The salon you met him at, that's his wife's salon! I only know because my sister used to work there, and say how much of a hoe he was. And now he done got my girl caught up in some mess, what you need me to do?"

"That's just it, I don't know! I'm about to leave to go home now." Renee said.

"Okay, come pick me up on 7th at the corner store, I'll go home with you. This nigga ain't about to do nothing to you or your baby, not with me around!"

Jr., Renee thought, she can't take him home with this crazy man lurking.

What can she tell her parents? There was no excuse to leave him, he had to go to school in the morning.

"Jay, give me about an hour, I'm going to call Michelle to see if Jr. can spend the night there I can't have my baby around this." They hung up, and Renee said her goodbyes to her family and they headed back to Frederick.

Renee had called Michelle before she left and gave her the run down. Of course, Michelle was all in and waiting for Jr. "Alright baby, Mommy will see you after school tomorrow ok," Renee said to Jr. as she dropped him off with Michelle.

"Okay mommy!" he gave her a kiss and hug.

"I got him Renee, be careful, you don't know what that crazy Bastard is capable of," said Michelle.

"I will, love ya girl." She walked away.

Renee scooped up Jay and headed to the apartment. They didn't know if Evan would be waiting outside or what. As they got out of the car, they made their way into her apartment.

Nothing was out of order, which she didn't think so because of the new locks. She pressed the answering machine. It had 66 messages and every one was Evan. Jay and Renee listened to each message. All of them were threats, threats, and more threats.

"Renee, this nigga is crazy!" Jay said. Renee just began to shake her head and cry. She was so upset at herself for letting herself get involved with someone like this.

"Why you crying? It's going to be ok!" said Jay. "No Jay, this is crazy. I should have never taken a dime from him! He feels like he owns me now, like I am his property!" Renee said.

Jay held Renee and they walked to the living room. "Girl you ain't perfect, you didn't know that nigga was crazy," they both busted up laughing. He was right, she didn't know he was crazy and she didn't know he was married. Better yet, Evan didn't know that SHE knew he was married.

"I think I have a solution to all this," said Renee.

"Girl, I hope you do, 'cause I don't wanna have to cut a nigga!" Jay said.

"No, listen. Evan doesn't know that I now know he is married, right? He thinks he's smart, but he is really dumb. He has left all these messages talking about what he has given me, the sex we had, what he was going to do to me, etc. What would he do if I gave a copy of these messages to his wife?"

"Girl, I think we got a plan," Jay said.

Evans wife was the bread winner. She had her salon and was very wealthy on her own through inheritance. She didn't need Evan.

From what Jay said, she was staying with him because he did whatever she said, and they had a kid together. Yes, he had his club, but her money made that club. Renee wouldn't really give his wife the tape unless he really would not leave her alone.

"I just want to move now, I want to go somewhere no one knows me!" she said.

"No, Renee. What would I do without my homie?" said Jay. "Boy please! I would be a phone call away." They burst into laughter at the same time the phone rang.

"Hello," Renee said.

"Well, look who decided to answer her phone. You know I lost a lot of money the other night at the club. You didn't show, and neither did Gigi or Shannon." Evan said. Renee couldn't care less. Gigi and Shannon were not reliable anyhow, they were always high when they were there.

"Evan, I'm done! This is not for me and neither is the so-called relationship." Renee said.

"Renee, as I said before, I wasn't going to hit you, you know that." Evan said.

"Dude, you slammed me up against glass and made my head bleed! That definitely will never happen again!" Renee said.

"Oh, so you're big and bad now, I'm coming over!" Evan said.

"NO, you're not! Evan it's over. Don't call, page me, or ever come to my house again!"

"You want to come bust my windows out you paid for go right ahead! I am over it! You want the clothes and jewelry back, I will leave it at the front door!" Renee felt a sense of relief. Jay was giving her the high five signs while listening.

"It's not over till I say it's over! What the hell?! You got a lot of balls now, compared to last time I saw you!" "What, you got some nigga telling you what to do now?!" Renee was silent. She knew when Evan said certain things that sounded too close to the truth, he was around.

"Where are you Evan?" Renee said, while peeping
out her kitchen window.

"Yeah bitch! I see everything! I saw you and that big nigga walk into your apartment. You got back up huh!" Evan said. For a minute, Renee was like, this man is not going to leave her alone. "Evan what do you want? I don't think your wife would appreciate you stalking me when you should be home with your family!" Evan was silent, "Don't worry about my damn wife, I got that!"

He didn't even deny that, he had really fed Renee a truck load of lies. Jay grabbed the phone, "Look nigga, my cousin is through with you! Now you can leave her alone, or we can tell your wife what you been up to! I am sure she would love to hear these tapes, she probably could make a good case in divorce court!"

The phone was silent, Renee grabbed the phone back. "Hello!" she said.

"You know what bitch, fuck you! I was trying to make you into a woman! Keep that shit, I don't want or need you! You were just another dumb bitch I could use!" Evan hung up, and at the same time they heard tires screech in the parking lot. He was gone.

Really, that's all it took? Renee didn't know if it was Jay getting in on the call, or the part about his wife. Whatever it was, she was glad it scared him enough to say he didn't want her. All that other stuff he said didn't faze her, she knew who she was.

After that night, Renee would see Evan every now and then. He would drive past her apartment at night here and there, but that was it. He never tried to contact her or harm her in anyway. Things could of took a turn for the worse she thought, if she had never reached out to Jay.

Chapter 7
DC IN THE HOUSE

"Last box, weeehooooo!" said Renee. She had done it. With help from Jay and other friends, she moved to Riverdale MD, about 10 minutes from DC. It was towards the end of summer. She had found a preschool for Jr. and landed a job at Howard University Hospital as a Medical Data Specialist. Her parents weren't happy she was moving even further away, but it wasn't too far. She was about an hour and a half away now.

She had a cousin who lived in the area, but other than that she didn't know no one. She wanted it that way, and she wanted a new beginning. She wanted to forget the bad stuff, especially the abortion. That was still bothering her, she would think about it daily. She had told herself, if she was ever in that predicament again, she would not go through another abortion no matter what.

It was the summer, so her parents would take Jr. for a month to spend more time with him. She had three more weeks before he came back. Her new job started this coming week. She had no time for games. She was no longer on housing, and was paying full rent at $700. She knew she could do it, she was going to be making good money, and she just had to budget.

Renee wasn't in town for two weeks before she met Adrian. He was a very nice guy, different completely. He was a DC guy. These men had a whole type of other swag to them. She had met him after visiting a Jamaican night club with one her cousins and high school friend from Gettysburg.

Adrian took Renee to places she never been. He even taught her how to eat with the correct silverware. She really didn't know what a salad fork was or anything. In Gettysburg, you didn't have fancy restaurants like DC/VA, not even in Frederick. He took her to the White House, she was amazed at what she saw. And when they made love, it was like a romantic movie. He would light candles, play soft music, and touch her so softly. She lived for that. She always wanted to feel like she was adored. She hadn't felt like that since she was with Ty. Some men just had a way of making you feel like a woman, and Adrian did that for her.

He still lived at home with his mom, and worked at a car dealership detailing cars during the day. Renee would get off work and chill at his house, or he would meet her at her house.

"Hey, so my son is going to be back next week. When he comes back, I really don't want him to so see you around, you will have to come at night." Renee told Adrian.

"I can respect that, and I respect you even more as women for doing that.

"You have girls that just don't care and have every man around their kids," said Adrian.

"I have not had the best relationships with men in the past. I don't want my son getting attached to someone, and it not work out." Renee said. Her and Adrian agreed, and then went back to watching T.V.

It was Monday morning, Renee dropped off Jr. at his new preschool, and off to work she went. She loved her job. She had started along with another girl named Kaz. They became instant friends. Kaz had no kids. She was smart and born and raised in DC. She knew all the best eating places and shopping spots. Renee and Kaz talked all day at work, and then went home talking about what happened at work. They stayed on the phone till late at night, and were up early in the morning.

Howard University was the spot, the place to be. Puffy Daddy and the Family would do concerts. All type of singers would perform at Howard, and the Jerk Chicken was to die for in DC.

Life was good, months had passed, and Renee was doing well with paying rent. Her bills were getting paid on time. She had even made another good friend in the apartments where she lived named Angela. Angela had a son the same age as Jr. so they would play with each other while Renee and Angela chilled.

Angela was from DC too, she was not to be played with. She was older than Renee and always gave her good advice. Angela worked in Virginia. Renee could only really see her on weekends. With traffic through the week she would get home too late.

Adrian was still around, and now had met Jr. That was a big step for Renee. She felt it was good for him. Jr's dad was still not in his life, and he needed a male figure. Her brother was very young, and her father was there, but he needed someone where she was. Adrian was great with Jr. They went to the park weekly. Adrian would walk with Renee, and Jr. was right in the middle. Renee never called Adrian her boyfriend, he was just her friend.

Renee felt it was time for him to meet her family. They had been dating for close to five months now, they both had an understanding about the relationship. They were not dating other people, just each other. But they were not official. They were taking their time and having fun. When Jr. was home, Adrian never stayed overnight. He would leave before Jr. woke up.

Renee's truck was in the shop one weekend, and it was the weekend that Jr. was supposed to come to her parents. She thought this would be the perfect time for them to meet Adrian.

He was down for it. Besides she had met his mom a long time ago. They pulled up in the driveway of her parents' home. Jr. was sleep in the back, "Ok, you ready?" she said. "Yeah, I'm good," said Adrian.

Renee didn't tell Adrian how big her father was. Adrian was the same height as Renee, but he was a small framed guy. He reached in the back and picked up Jr.

Renee opened her parent's door, her brother and sister ran toward her. "Jr. is here!" They were smiling from ear to ear, they loved their nephew. "Hi!" said Renee. As her mom and dad came around the corner. "This is Adrian!" Renee said while waking up Jr. Adrian shook her father's hand, then her mother's. They all made small talk in the kitchen, then Adrian and Renee took off back to Maryland.

"You did not tell me your dad was so big, he looks like Danny Glover!" they burst into laughter. He did look like Danny Glover, he was told that all the time. "Well, I didn't want you to be all scared and all, that's why!" Renee said. Adrian looked at Renee and laughed some more, as they made their way back home.

Renee's dad really didn't say too much to Renee about Adrian. Renee didn't bring too many guys around. She was always afraid of what her dad would say. Every time he said what he thought was wrong with the men, he would be right. She was in shock when he didn't say anything negative about Adrian.

Granted, he only met him for a brief 20 minutes, the only question he asked was, "Where he work?"

"He works at a car dealership, detailing cars!" said Renee.

"How did he get that BMW? He must sell drugs or something?" her father asked while sucking on a toothpick.

"No dad! That's one of the cars at the dealership he drives!" she said. Then he nodded his head and continued to look at T.V.

The New Year had come and gone, and Renee was still working at Howard. She and Adrian were still seeing each other, but Adrian was going back and forth to Atlanta. He was offered a job there and came back to DC once a month. They were still close, but had decided to date outside of each other. It wouldn't have been fair not to.

Jr. was getting bigger and starting look more like his daddy, who was still MIA. Renee hadn't received a dime of child support since he was born. Ryan was either in jail or going back to jail. He never tried to contact Renee to see his son at all. It was ok, Jr. was doing just fine. He had his grandfather to look up to, and that's all he needed.

Renee's sister, Taylor had moved to Frederick now to live with her new husband. So, she had family even closer now.

Renee was just leaving the house one morning with Jr. when she ran into a gentleman outside her front door. Renee did not have time for this, she was running late and still had to drop Jr. off. He was dressed in a janitor's uniform with a hat to the side. He was older, gray goatee, and dark skinned. He was about two inches shorter than Renee. "Ah, I'm sorry beautiful. What's your name?" he said.

"Hi, I'm Renee. I'm sorry, but I am in a hurry!" she said while trying to pass.

"I'm sorry, my name is Kevin." He said "Hi, uh Kevin is it? Nice to meet you. Have a good day!" she yelled out while running to her car.

She did not have time for no weak ass sorry line from no one. She was about her money. She had to get to work.

"Girl, then he was really trying to run game with that janitor uniform on!" Renee said to Kaz. "No, he didn't! Girl these guys are too much!" Kaz said. Renee wasn't picky, as she would say, but she was not giving the time of day to the man that fixed toilets.

Later that evening, as Renee and Jr. were making their way up to her apartment, she found a note on her door.

Hello Beautiful, I know you were in a hurry this morning, but I wanted to introduce myself again. My name is Kevin. I am the Maintenance Manager for these properties.

I am not stalking you, but I want to know if I could take you out. I have left my number below, call me if you like. If not, I will understand no love lost. Promise.

Kevin

555-555-5555

"Really!" Renee said out loud. "Really!" Jr. mocked her, and she began to laugh.

It was two days later. Renee had just laid Jr. down for a nap, and was cleaning the kitchen table when she picked up the note again. "Hell, why not!" she said.

"Hello," the voice said.

"Hello is this Kevin?" Renee said

"Yes, this is him. This must be Renee?" he said.

"How did you know it was me?" she said.

"I remember that voice," he said. They talked for hours just getting to know each other. Kevin was 42, 20 years her senior. He had a daughter from a previous relationship, and lived in Silver Springs Maryland, a couple minutes from where she lived. He had been working for the same company for a while and had just been promoted. They didn't have anything really in common, besides kids. He had been to jail before for something small when he was younger. She decided to give him a chance, and go out on a date with him. They went to dinner while Angela watched Jr. for the night, so she could get out. It was cool. They ate, then went to the movies.

This went on for a couple months. On the weekends, Renee's parents had Jr. She stayed at Kevin's house. They would dance, play cards, and smoke weed till late at night. "What the hell are you doing?" Kevin said as he watched Renee puff on the joint. "Dang, girl puff, puff, give!" he said. Months had passed, and Renee and Kevin were a couple now. Adrian would still call her and check up on her, and he would come over and spend time with Jr. They had made a bond, even though Adrian and Renee were not spending time together like before. That never stopped their friendship, he understood her and she understood him. She knew if she ever needed him, he would be there.

One-day Renee was alone at Kevin's house. She had gotten off early and decided to stop by. She had a key to his apartment now. As she opened the door and walked through the house, she went to the kitchen to grabbed a coke. While there the phone rang, she was not going to answer, the answering machine picked up.

"I don't know why you ain't returning my calls, you ain't shit! You can't even keep your promises! You said you were going to bring me that money, and you haven't shown up yet! This is the last time I am calling. The next step is taking you to court for child support."

"You think you can come give me money when you want and have sex to make it all better, I got something for you!"

Renee couldn't believe her ears. For one he is not taking care of his child-like he said he was, and two he's still sleeping with this chick! She was so angry she slammed the can onto the counter and began to text Kevin." Where are you!" "Coming around the corner." "Ok, I'm here!" She didn't know what she was going to say," Hey beautiful," he said as he kissed her on the cheek.

"Hey, you might want to check your messages, you just had and important call!" she said.

Kevin grabbed a beer and pressed the play button. It was complete silence from him as the message played. Renee stood in front of him with her arms folded.

"What?" he said. "That bitch is lying! I ain't slept with her in ages, since about a year after my daughter was born!"

Renee didn't say anything, "wow," she thought. He didn't say nothing about not taking care of his child. He was so focused on her not believing he had sex with his ex. At that moment, she had a flash back to Jr's father. She didn't want to be with a man who didn't take care of his child.

"I don't know what to believe! She sounded like she was mad. You haven't been taking care of your child?" she said. "Renee, this bitch is mad cause I ain't with her, she will say anything!" "I take care of my child, she's full of shit!" Kevin put his arms around her. "Don't let her mess up what we have. I need you

Renee, you give me life, and I love us together." Renee just stared at him. They were together every day; how could he be sleeping with her. Even on the weekends when he had his daughter, he would bring her to Renee's house to play with Jr.

Renee leaned in and kissed Kevin on the lips. "I believe you, but you need to take it to court and let them handle it!" Kevin didn't reply, he just began kissing Renee and they made their way to the bedroom. They made love for over an hour, just enjoying themselves. In the middle of making love Kevin whispered "Renee, I love you, in her ear." Renee responded "I love you too." She had never said that to anyone. They were moving fast! The next day Kevin took her to go meet his mother.

"Hello, you must be Renee?" His mother said. Kevin was a male version of his mother. She was gorgeous, light skinned, and had hair like Della Reese.

"Hello, I am Renee."
"Come have a seat, come talk to me!" she said. They chatted about Renee past, her parents, and Jr.

Then his mother asked, "Let me ask you something. Why are you with my son?" Renee was in shock. "Well," Renee said. "I don't mean to bombard you, but he is 20 years older than you. I just want to know what you two have in common." She made a good point. Renee thought if that was my son, I would want to know too.

"Well, I love him for who he is. I enjoy just spending time with him. We talk about everything and I can be myself." Renee said.

His mother smiled and said "Ok, if he's happy, I'm happy!" then she smiled again. Renee was relieved. Kevin had made his way back into the room by this time. "Is everything ok?" he asked. Renee and his mother both nodded their head and smiled. Kevin and Renee said their goodbyes and they left. Renee thought, Kevin is really serious if he took her to meet his mother. Men don't just take anyone to meet their mother. They have to be special, she thought. She then looked over at Kevin while he was driving and gave him a kiss.

"What's that for?" he said. "Just being you," said Renee.

It was the New Year Eve of 1999. Renee wanted to bring in the New Year in Gettysburg at her parents'. She had told her parents about Kevin, they were going to meet him for the first time.

They arrived at her parents' house just before 10pm New Year's Eve. Jr. was sleep; so, she put him in the bed with her brother who was already passed out.

"Mom, Dad, this is Kevin," she said. Her father looked Kevin up and down and shook his hand. Her mother said "Hello."

Renee knew by the look in her father's eye, he was not impressed. Renee's father and Kevin made small talk in the living room while Renee and her mother were in the kitchen. Renee's mother looked over at her.

"What?"

"I didn't say anything. You know your dad is going to find out everything he can about him. I can already tell he don't like him!" Renee looked over, and then shrugged her shoulders. What could she say, her father was going to say something regardless if she liked it or not.

Midnight struck, and they toasted the New Year with glasses of Champagne that Kevin had brought along to impress her parents. After the toast, Renee's mother fixed Kevin a plate of food she had cooked. Renee's father asked her to come in the basement, he had something he wanted to show her. Once they had gotten down there, Raymond started in. "I don't like him!" he said. "Why dad?" said Renee. "He thinks he's too smooth, and he thinks he's young. He almost old as me, and got his pants hanging off his butt like a young cat!"

"I listened to him talk the whole time, he trying to be something he's not!" Renee just shook her head. What could she say, Kevin did wear his pants like that and he did talk like that.

"And why you want to date someone that old, anyway?" he said.

"I like him Daddy, a lot!" Renee "Well mark my words, it ain't going to work. He still trying to act like a young buck. I'm just saying!" Renee nodded, and they headed back upstairs. Well, Renee thought, no one will never be good enough for him, she had to come to realize that.

A couple minutes later, they left to go to a local hotel nearby. The one rule in her parents' home was, you were not laying up in their house unmarried.

That night Kevin and Renee made love all night, drank Champagne, and smoked Newport's. Renee didn't smoke cigarettes a lot, but she smoked when she was with Kevin. "Renee, I really love you, you know, that, right?" Kevin said. "I love you too Kevin!"

Little did she know that January 1, 2000 would change the rest of her life as she knew it.

Chapter 8

PREGNANCY #3

"OMG!" Renee looked in the mirror at herself, then down at the pregnancy test. She was pregnant. Another child! She didn't know what to do. How was she going to tell Kevin? He was much older than her. She wanted to be with him, but a child was not in the picture. They had only been dating for about six months, not enough time to know everything, she thought. Well, she had to tell him. She had to be at least a month now, it was mid-February 2000. This meant that the baby was conceived on New Year's night, and honestly, it probably was. They had gotten wasted that night when they got to the hotel. Renee knew this time she was not going through another abortion. She had told herself the last time that it was not going to happen again. It would be ok. Jr. will be five soon, and the baby would have a good age gap between them.

"Hey, beautiful, what ya doing?" said Kevin over the phone. Renee was just finishing up some cleaning around the house.

"Nothing much. Hey, can you come by?" she said.

"I am right around the corner; I'll be there soon." He said.

Kevin was there within minutes. Jr was still at school. So, Renee thought this would be the perfect time to tell Kevin the news. She walked back and forth throughout her apartment. She was nervous. This was not planned at all. All she could think about is, it doesn't matter how he feels, this is my body.

Knock, Knock!

"Come in" said Renee.

"Hey Renee, what's up?" Kevin said as he hugged her.

"Sit down. Look I know we only been dating for a while and all, but I am-"

"Pregnant!" Kevin said.

"How did you know?" said Renee. Kevin sat back, and took his hat off his head.

"Renee, I didn't. I just knew when you said you had to talk to me, that was it. So, what are we going to do? I really don't want another kid, but it's your choice, I will be there for you either way," said Kevin.

Renee was silent. She knew what her choice was going to be.

"I am going to have this baby, I cannot have an abortion!"

"Ok, well, we're having a baby!" said Kevin. Just like that, it was done. There was not another conversation about it.

Couple months had gone by and Renee was now six months pregnant.

She had gone down south with Kevin, and met some more members of his family. He had an uncle that passed away that he was close too. They started to become closer than ever, and then after a while, they slowly drifted apart. Kevin was around, but it wasn't like before.

Renee had found out recently that he was still seeing his baby's mother. His child's mother had called Renee one night after she heard Renee was pregnant. She told her of all the times they hooked up. Which was true because those were the nights that Kevin was not with her. Renee started to not care about him anymore. She had told herself, "I'm going to have this baby, and take care of him/her just like I've been doing with Jr!" That was one thing she knew how to do, is take care of her own, without a man. Sure, she would have wanted the family life, but it was not going to be. Just like her father had said, Kevin was still running the streets like a young buck.

He would still stay the night, and she still had a key to his house. They would of course still have sex, that was her baby's father, but now she was making sure he wore condoms. She of course, still had her family, although they didn't care for Kevin. Her parents were happy about having another grandchild. So was Jr. He was so excited, he couldn't wait! Every day he was rubbing her stomach, waiting for the baby to kick.

Around this time, Renee was using dating websites in her free time to meet new people. Not to have a relationship or anything, just someone to talk to. She had lots of hits, all good-looking men, but that didn't matter because she wasn't really trying to go there. There was one man, named Paul. He was good looking (at least in the pictures). He had two children, and worked as a truck driver. He lived a couple towns over. They emailed every now and then, they never met or talked on the phoned, they just spoke online. He knew about Renee's situation, and she knew about his at this time. It was just someone to talk to that she felt didn't judge her, and was sincere.

"So, we need to talk about what's going to happen when the baby gets here," said Renee.

"What you mean? I already told you, I'm going to be there for you, and do what I can!" said Kevin.

"What you can?"

"Yeah, Renee. I have another child. I have to also pay rent and a car note too!"

Was he really going this route now, acting like this baby wasn't going to be here soon? He had all this time to get his shit right, Renee thought. They had nothing at this time. No baby bed, clothes, diapers, nothing. She knew her parents were going to help, but that was not their responsibility.

"We have nothing Kevin! This baby will be here in less than a month!" she screamed

"Renee, you the one wanted this baby. You should have thought of all this!" Kevin screamed back.

Renee was heated! She and Kevin went back and forth until Jr. came out of his room.

"Go back to bed Jr., it's ok, we're just talking." said Renee. Jr. turned around and went back in his room and closed the door.

Renee and Kevin looked at each other and sat down on the couch.

"Look Kevin, I am not asking you to do everything, I just want to co-parent. If you can pay for daycare, that will be fine. I will take care of everything else, and we won't have to get child support involved!"

Renee was serious. That's all she needed was him to pay for daycare. She was going to send the baby to the same place Jr. goes for before and after care. They were responsible, and she felt her kids were safe with that babysitter.

"I can do that Renee. I am sorry I yelled. I'm just frustrated my job is tripping, it just has me stressed." They hugged; and then watched some TV and went to bed.

Dear Diary,

It's been awhile huh, well now another baby is on the way! This time I am not even thinking about abortion. If the father cannot do his part, I must do what I have to do to get by. Even though I don't go to church, maybe there is a God, and he is giving me a second chance because of the abortion. I will be 23 years old with two kids, $700 dollar's in rent, not including the other bills. It would help if Kevin would help, but I am not going to rely on him. I just pray I have everything ready for this little one before he/she comes. Alright, all for now, I must rise and shine early!

The next day, Renee and Kevin were up and off by 7:30 am. Kevin went to his job, and Renee went to her work. She was getting all her paperwork for her maternity leave. It was going to be hard for the two months she was taking off. She had $700 rent to pay, and not to mention the other bills in her home. It was going to be tight, which meant she was going to have to shop smart. She was making her list for the grocery store, when Kaz interrupted her.

"Hey, you ready to eat? I brought you some food!" said Kaz.

"Girl, now you know the answer to that!" Renee said as she followed Kaz to the break room.

"Surprise!" yelled all her coworkers. It was a small office of about 10 people, but they had the entire break room filled with baby gifts. Renee began to cry. She was so thankful, she couldn't stop crying. She had gotten clothes, bottles, baby food, a swing, and a carrier that she needed. And one coworker got her a six- month supply of diapers. She couldn't help but to burst out in tears. Kaz had helped plan the shower. She spoke to Renee every night, and she knew she had nothing for the baby.

"I don't know how to thank you guys!" Renee whelped.

"You don't have to thank us, you are one of us, this is our gift to you!" said her boss.

They all gave her a hug, and started to eat. They had Jamaican food, American food, all types; you name it. It was like a feast, all the food you can eat!

She was set! Her parents had gotten her the rest of the odds and ends. She had gotten a crib from a friend who had previously had a baby, and didn't need it anymore. Kevin had come over that night and helped put it together.

"Let's go on the balcony," said Kevin. "What's up?" said Renee. She knew something was up when Kevin said let's go to the balcony. That was where they smoked cigarettes and weed. Kevin lit up a joint, he puffed a couple hits, then said, "I quit my job today."

"What?" said Renee. She was furious! "How could you do something so stupid, and we have a baby on the way."

"They were on my ass for nothing. I cussed out the owner and walked out." "It was that bitch!" he said.

"What are you talking about?"
"My baby's mother kept calling my job about some damn child support, and my boss came at me telling me to get my shit together!" "I told him to stay the fuck out of my business and walked out!" Renee just stared at him. He couldn't be that stupid she thought.

"Kevin, we have a baby on the way, I need your help!"

"Damn Renee, what about my feelings, it's always the baby, the baby, the baby. I come to you telling you my problem, that's all you can say? I know WE have a baby on the way, shit!" Kevin was screaming now.

Renee screamed back. "Hell yes, it's about the baby, the baby, the baby. You helped create this child just like me. I am standing up to my responsibilities, what you did doesn't even make sense, just stupid. You're almost 43 years old, you too damn old to be acting like a fucking 20-year-old boy!" Renee was livid. Was he sitting here talking about how he walked out on a job cause his boss told him to get his shit together? His boss should have said that thought Renee. He needs to get his shit together, he's too damn old for this!

Keven got right up into Renee's face almost touching her nose. "Who the fuck you talking to bitch, I don't have to do shit for you! I only agreed to have this baby because YOU wanted it. I don't need another child!" Spit was flying everywhere as he was talking. Renee just stared at him; everything her father said was coming true once again. This wasn't a man; this was a young boy in a man's body.

"Get out!" Renee screamed as she opened the front door. She was starting to have contractions with all the yelling. She needed him out!

"Fuck you!" Kevin yelled, as he walked out. Renee went to her room to lie down on her bed, and begin to cry. All her past relationships went through her mind. She was so upset at herself. How could she let another man do this to her? How could she have been so careless when having sex?

She thought about Ty. If she only had told him how she was feeling, that she wanted to build a life with him., maybe she wouldn't be in this position she is in now. Out of all the guys she dated, Ty was the only one who she wanted. She realized all these years, she was playing different men, and trying to find one like him. It was too late now. She had heard from her cousin Sarah a month ago, that Ty was in a serious relationship, and possibly had a baby on the way. Why was she even thinking about him?

He wouldn't want her now with two kids and two baby daddies? That's too much baggage she thought for any man. For the next couple days, Renee kept to herself. She went to work, came home, spent time with Jr., then off to bed they went. The only person she spoke to was Paul and Kaz. Kaz was her support. She always told her, "Girl you don't need no man, you got this. It may be hard, but you going to be alright!" Paul would say basically the same thing when they spoke. They began to talk daily on the phone now, and they were getting closer. Renee had concluded that she was going to be raising two kids alone. She started getting the remaining items she needed here and there. She started paying some of her bills ahead of time to be on track. Her due date was just around the corner; she was going to be off eight weeks. Four out of the eight weeks she was not going to be paid. She got set up on a budget plan for her electric and gas, so that helped. Now her focus was rent and food.

October 3, 2000, it was a Tuesday night about 9pm. Renee was home with Jr. She was counting contractions; they were getting closer and closer. She did not know what to do. She had a baby sitter for Jr., but what about Kevin. They hadn't spoken since that night on the balcony. Renee didn't want to be with him, but she wasn't going to keep the birth of his child away from him.

"Hello," Kevin said.

"Hey, Kevin I think I'm going into labor. Can you come take me to the Hospital!"

"Yeah, I will be there in a minute," said Kevin.

Renee began to get Jr. dressed. He was going to stay at the neighbors, and they would send him off to school in the morning.

The contractions began to get stronger. Renee looked down at her phone, and it was over 40 minutes. "Where the hell is he!" she said out loud. Kevin lived a good 10 minutes away. It does not take that long! A couple minutes late, Kevin was at the door ready to go. He reeked of brandy and marijuana. His eyes were red, and he wouldn't look Renee in the face. How could he come here high and smelling of liquor? Their baby was about to be born, and the first person he is going to see is a drunken father!

"Well, you're not dilated at all, but contractions are getting there. Why don't you go home and walk it out, then come back when contractions are at least 15 minutes apart," said the ER doctor.

"Are you serious!" said Renee. The hospital was about 20 minutes away. She was feeling the same way she was feeling when she was in labor with Jr. Renee was not going home, she had already made up her mind.

"Let's just go, we can come back when they get closer Renee," said Kevin. He was trying to sound so concerning in front of the doctor. Renee knew that was an act. Kevin hadn't text or nothing to ask about how she was doing since the night they had the argument. Renee began to put on her clothes, and met Kevin in the waiting area outside. "I am not going home. This baby is coming. I want to stay here and walk it out!" she told Kevin.

"Well, I have plans, you can stay here then. If they don't admit you, call me back and I will pick you up." He said. Renee just stared at him. She couldn't believe the words coming out of his mouth. This was not the man she knew months ago. "Whatever, do you then Kevin, I will call you then!"

She turned around and walked off. Renee walked around the entire hospital several times. She passed other women in early labor walking with their spouses. She longed to have that partner that could be by her side like that. Even if Kevin had just stayed, he didn't have to walk with her, he still would be there for her.

It was now midnight. Renee had been texting Kevin with no response. What was she going to do now? She didn't want to call Kaz, she lived in inner DC area. Renee was way on the other side of PG County at the hospital. She then called her doctor and explained to him what the ER doctor had said. He phoned the hospital and had her admitted.

After being admitted a couple of hours later, Renee had fallen to sleep. She awoke up in extreme pain. While she was asleep, the nurses had started her on Pitocin to get her contractions more regular. "AWWWWWWWEEEEE, IT'S HURTING!" she screamed. Renee was fully dilated. She had been asleep longer than she thought. The room was full. There were four nurses, two pediatric doctors, and her doctor. Renee had been fully dilated for at least 20 minutes. She would not push. She could feel every pain that you feel when giving natural birth, but 10 times worse. They had called the team in because they were afraid the baby would not make it.

"Renee, I need you to push this baby out please!" screamed her doctor.

"I can't it hurts, AAHHHHHHHHHHHHH!" she screamed. "Give me the forceps we have to get this baby out!" screamed the doctor. "Renee, please push!"

Renee looked up, and pushed as much as she could. Slowly, with the help of the forceps, the baby came out. Splitting Renee's vagina almost in half. They rushed the baby over to the incubator to make sure he was ok. The baby was fine. It was a boy! They pushed the baby over to Renee's side in the incubator as they were checking him. He looked over at Renee with his eyes wide open, and their eyes connected.

He was perfect! They stared at each other for a while. Renee could see her family traits in his eyes and nose. He was sucking his fist, and not making a sound. Renee thought to herself, you're finally here! "What's this little fellow name going to be?" asked the nurse.

"ANTHONY ISAIAH JACKSON!" said Renee, while smiling at him.

"Renee, I had to do a lot of stitching. You were ripped pretty good. How are you feeling?" asked the doctor. "I am OK now. I'm so sorry I put you all through that. I just couldn't push" she said.

"You don't need to apologize, he is here and healthy, and you are fine. That's all that matters"

Anthony Jackson was born October 4, 2000 at 10:45am, weighing 6 lbs. 9 ounces.

Kevin never came back to the hospital. Renee left messages, and the nurses called when the baby was coming. No response. A couple hours after the baby was born, Renee's sister Taylor and mother walked in. They got in the car and headed to the hospital immediately after the hospital had called stating Renee was about to have the baby. Renee's family stayed for a little, then headed to the school to pick up Jr. Her parents were going to watch him for the rest of the week while Renee went home and got situated.

Later that day, Kevin paid a visit to the hospital.

"What happened to you? I called you several times!" said Renee

"I didn't hear my phone," Kevin said as he picked up the baby. "Why is he so small?" he said.

"He's not, Kevin. He's an average size newborn," she said while shaking her head.

Kevin stayed for a little while longer, and then he started getting ready to leave.

"Are you going to be able to take us home tomorrow?" she asked.

"No, can't you call one of your friends? I have to work tomorrow." he said.

Renee was boiling inside. She laid back and looked up at the ceiling. "So, you got a new job?" she said.

"No, I talked to my boss and got my job back," he said.

"It's fine. I will call a friend." She was done. First, he didn't come to the birth, and then he couldn't even take her home. Renee knew then she was done with Kevin, even if he tried to slick his way back in. She was never going to let him come back. He already showed Anthony how much he cared. She phoned one of her friends to pick her and Anthony up the next day.

Dear Diary,

He's here, and he's perfect! My baby boy, and now there is two. I went through this delivery alone, one of the scariest times of my life. I felt so alone, how could a man leave his baby's mother alone? He is no man at all, just a sperm donor! I am a 23-year-old woman with two kids now. I have a lot of responsibilities on my own. I will work two jobs if I have to, to provide for my children. It's us against the world. God has given me another baby, I guess God has forgiven me for the abortion. Thank you!

Chapter 9
TWO KIDS AND A FIANCE

It had been over a month now, and Anthony was doing great. He was sleeping through the night at two months old well, at least five hours at a time. Renee was relieved. She spent her days taking care of Anthony and talking to Paul on the phone. Then when Jr. came home from school, she would help him with his homework and watch a little TV with him. She was getting the hang of having two kids.

She was about to go back to work next week and had applied for daycare help through the local welfare office. They had a program for single mothers that helped with childcare if they worked, something she learned from having Jr. And if they could help her now, she was going to use it.

Kevin hadn't done anything. He started calling the week Renee got home late at night to come see the baby. Renee was not fooled. No one wants to see a baby at midnight, he just wanted sex, and Renee wasn't having it at all! He bought a couple bags of diapers, and that was basically it. She had to borrow money from her father for the first time in her life while she was off work to pay her rent. She was embarrassed.

She was determined to do whatever it took to make it. She tried to apply for food stamps, but they denied her because she would not file child support on Kevin. She wanted to give him every chance to do what he said he was going to do. She needed to talk to him, if he was not going to help, then she needed to take her next steps.

Ring, Ring. "Hey Kevin, I need to talk to you about Anthony." She said. "I will be over tonight," he said. "OK, Kevin can you try to come before 9, I don't want to be up late," she said. Kevin agreed and hung up. Later that night, there was a knock at the door. It was 11:00pm. He has no respect at all, she thought, as she answered the door. "Where's the baby?" he said.

"He's asleep Kevin, its 11pm," she said, whispering. Kevin sat at the kitchen table.

"I need to know if you're going to help or not?" said Renee. She looked him straight in the face, with no expression.

"I told you I would. Damn, that's what you called me over here for?" he said.

"Yes, I did. I have to go back to work next week. His daycare is going to be $350 a month. I can't pay that and everything else he needs!" she raised her voice. "The only other choice I have is to take you for child support, if you don't."

"Well, I guess you need to go file for child support then, because I don't have no $350 for you!"

Renee was enraged. "Are you serious, I thought we made an agreement, you tell me now, a couple days before I have to be back to work!"

"I want a blood test too, I ain't paying for no more kids that ain't mine!" Kevin had found out while Renee was pregnant, his child he had been taking care of for three years was not his. Understandable, but Renee wasn't just any chick. You could not separate them around the time when she conceived, and on top of that he waits till now to start this? This started an intense argument that quickly turned physical with Kevin. Renee was left with bruises on her face and arms. She was heartbroken, things got physical, quick. She was not going to be walking around scared like she did years ago, in Frederick. If a man swung on her, she was going to defend herself the best way she could, and that's what she did. She cleaned herself up and immediately checked on the kids. She picked Anthony up from his crib, and walked over to the window with him and began to cry out loud.

"I am so sorry Anthony, I am so sorry! I wish that was not your daddy, but it is. Mommy will do everything in her power to protect you. You and your brother will never have to want for anything. Just like I never had to want for anything as a child. I am so sorry you have to be brought into this!"

Renee then returned Anthony back to his crib, and cried herself to sleep

The next day her friend Lisa took photos of her and took her to the court house to get a restraining order on Kevin. "Girl what happened, you look awful!" said Lisa "I don't even remember all of it. We were arguing over child support, and next thing I know we were swinging at each other!" Renee said. "This is not good Renee. Now what? How are you all going to co-parent, and you can't be near each other?" "We're not. He doesn't care about Anthony. I will raise him just like I'm raising Jr., ALONE! Just me and my boys, and that's ok with me," said Renee. It wasn't, but what was she going to say? She was going to get through this, she knew that for sure.

Court was next week, and Kevin was supposed to show for the judge to decide whether to enforce the order. Kevin never showed.

The judge hit his gravel, "As ordered, the defendant is a no show. Per pictures and evidence, your restraining order is granted for a year!" It was over just like that. The next place to go was public assistance to help with daycare. Renee had to delay going back to work for a week to get it all in order. She was granted a voucher for daycare that covered almost all childcare, except $100 a month, which she was responsible for. She was denied food stamps because she made too much (so the state says).

But she was going to be OK. She made enough to pay her bills. She would get short on food at times, but she went to food banks on Friday's at local churches, and that helped a lot. She was never a member at any of the churches. Not to say the members didn't try when she went to the food banks. But now, in her life, church wasn't a priority to her. She now believed God and Jesus was real, and prayed every now and then. That's where it stopped. She was given prayer pamphlets every time she went to the food banks. She would read about a page or two, then threw it away. Renee's thought at the time was, I'm OK. Life is fine. I don't need to know more about God right now.

Renee was so exhausted from all the crap she was going through, she just didn't feel like pursuing the child support at that time.

"Girl, are you crazy?" said Kaz

"I am going to do it, I'm tired Kaz, I am so exhausted! Yes, the money would help greatly, but I am so stressed out, you don't understand!" she began to cry.

"No, girl, I get it. But don't let him off easy. He made this child with you. He needs to own up and help. You out here busting your butt at work, and going home to two small kids every night. I don't see how you do it." Kaz shook her head.

"Those are my boys!!!" Renee smiled

The New Year had come and gone. It was now March 2001. Renee had just celebrated a birthday and Jr. was almost six years old. Anthony was growing quickly. He was now five months old and adorable. He looked just like his daddy. Renee still had the restraining order on Kevin, but he did see them in crossing twice. They didn't talk, he would hold Anthony when he saw him play a couple minutes, ask how Renee was, then give him back. She still hadn't filed child support on him. He had starting leaving diapers once in a while at the door. That was getting old though, he did nothing else.

Renee and Paul had finally met on New Year's at a friend's house. They were actively dating now. They had known each other since she was in the middle of her pregnancy. They practically knew all about each other. So, it was no surprise when he proposed to her on her birthday. Well at least to them. Her friends thought it was fast, but they did know each other for almost eight months now. There was not going to be a wedding anytime soon though. That was for sure! Renee and Paul wanted to make sure they were financially stable before that. Her parents were happy for her, and extremely happy that they were not rushing into marriage anytime soon.

"So, what you think, Dad?" Renee said to her father on a visit.

"It's your life, he seems OK. I need to feel him out a little more though." said Renee's father. There was something about him that Raymond couldn't put his finger on. But for the most part, he liked Paul, and so did her mother. Maybe it's because Renee didn't tell them the exact truth on how they met online. She had told her parents they had met at church. Well, they kind of did, if a Christian website counted. She was afraid to hear what they would say if she told them the truth. A lot of people frowned upon online dating because you didn't know if that was a real person who you were speaking to.

Paul lived in Laurel MD, which was about an hour from Renee. By this time, he had basically moved in. He would stay at her house part time and his mothers the other half. It was just easier, with the commuting back and forth. Renee had met his mom, sister, and his children. Paul did not have a good relationship with his baby's mothers at all. Not to mention he was in the middle of going through a divorce with the last baby mama. That was another reason they were waiting to get married. His mother and sister were very open to Renee and her kids. They treated them as if they were his kids, and Renee respected that. Paul is all Anthony knew as a father figure. He definitely didn't see his real father as one because he didn't know him.

Paul and Renee were alone for the weekend, and Renee's parents had the kids.

"You need to file child support on Anthony's father," said Paul, out the blue. Renee looked over at him. "What? I mean I know, but why are you bringing this up now?" she asked.

"Because it's not fair. Yes, I love Anthony as my own, but the reality is, someone helped you make him. He's not doing anything at all. You're too nice!"

"It's not that I am too nice, it's just I look at Jr., and I filed child support on his dad a couple months after he was born, and to this day I have received nothing. I went through the same thing, him wanting a blood test, it comes back 99.9% his, and he still doesn't want to do nothing. Granted, he has been in jail 80% of the time, but when he is out, he doesn't call or nothing. Then, when they finally track him down for child support, he goes back to jail for something else." Renee said.

"True, but that's Jr's Dad. Anthony's Dad works every day. He comes by and drops a bag of diapers here and there, and you just let him get away with it. I pay child support for both of my kids because that's what a man does, he should too!"

He was right, Renee thought. There is no reason why he cannot pay her child support. It could take care of the daycare, and that would be $100 less she needed to worry about.

She knew what he made an hour at his job, and how the state calculated it. So, he would probably be paying what she asked from him in the beginning. "You're right Paul, I am. He is 43 years old, and needs to help take care of his child." She looked at him.

That Monday, Renee called in to work and stated she was going to be late. She went and filled paperwork for child support. After she was done she felt a heavy weight off her shoulders. This is something that should have been done a long time ago. On the way to work her phoned ring.

"Hello!" she said.

"Hey Renee, this is Adrian, how are you?" She hadn't spoken to Adrian since before Anthony was born. Last, she spoke to him he was still in ATL.

"Hey, how are you Adrian, you still in Georgia?" she said.

"Actually, I am, but I'm in town for the week. I wanted to know if I could come by and see Jr. I have some videos for his game I want to give him." He said.

"Um, sure that's fine, but I should tell you, my finance might be there. I don't want it to be weird." She said. There was silence. "You're engaged? So, you decided to go ahead and stay with your baby's daddy?" Adrian sound surprised. Renee did not feel like telling Adrian the entire story, so she gave him the short version.

"Girl, you will never be alone, that's for sure!" They both started to laugh. "Come on Adrian, Paul is cool! We're not getting married tomorrow. We're going to wait about two years." She said. "It's all good. I will be there around six if that's ok?" said Adrian. "That's perfect, I will let Jr. know." They hung up.

Jr. was young, but he remembered Adrian. It probably was because all the time they spent together. Renee was sure he would be happy to see him, and get gifts! But what would Paul say? He never met Adrian, and he was coming over tonight. She didn't have time to think about it now, she had to get to work. She wasn't at work two hours before her cell phone rang, it was Paul.

"Hey, I am at the door!" he said. You couldn't just walk into her job. They had cameras on the door and a locked entry. It was down town DC, anything could happen. Howard University made sure they were safe. Renee started to get up, "Girl, where you going?" asked Kaz.

"Paul is at the door, probably with lunch!" She said. Kaz rolled her eyes, she didn't care for Paul too much, and neither did other people in the office. Kaz felt that Paul was pressuring Renee to marry him. Yes, Renee had already agreed, but something was just off with him. "Hey Kaz, how are you?" Paul asked as he followed Renee to her desk with a dozen of roses.

"I'm good, how are you?" Kaz said. "Good, Good. Hey Renee, I can't stay long my work truck is double parked, but I wanted to drop these off." Paul said. "Aww, they are so
pretty!" she said as she kissed him. "I need to talk to you, I will walk you out."

"Hey, so my ex Adrian, you remember me talking about him when we use to talk on line?"

"Vaguely, that was a while ago. What about him?"

"He is in town, and he wanted to see Jr. to bring him some games he got him for his game station." She said.

"Okay, when?" he said.

"Well, this evening, I told him about you and all."

"Renee, that's fine. I trust you, plus I will be there. I will see you later, I got to go," Paul was making his way inside his truck.

"Okay, see ya at home!" Renee yelled. Well, that
went better than she thought. She came back inside and told Kaz about the conversation.

Kaz stopped typing, and looked at Renee, "Girl, you mean to tell me your fiancé is letting your ex, who is not neither of your babies' daddy come over, and didn't say anything?"

"No, he said okay."

"Renee, he's got a side chick girl!" said Kaz.

"Why you say that? Where did that come from?" asked Renee.

"Renee come on, a nigga is not going to let another nigga especially an ex, who is not neither of your baby's father come and visit. What the hell?" Renee began to get angry with Kaz. "Kaz, not every man is a cheater! Just because you were cheated on, why do you always go there?"

Kaz stood up and started to raise her voice, "YOU KNOW WHAT!" then she stopped.

"Renee, just forget what I said. Don't pay me no mind. You're engaged to a man you met online and only known for a year. If that's what makes you happy, then it makes me happy." She walked away.

Renee didn't say a word, she didn't like when Kaz was upset at her. That was her confidant. Renee got up and followed Kaz.

"Kaz, stop I am sorry. I didn't mean that." Kaz had confided in Renee two times when she was cheated on by her ex. Renee knew it hurt Kaz.

"I respect what you say as my friend, but I love Paul and he loves me. I trust him. I don't want you to think I don't respect your advice." said Renee.

"NO, I am sorry! I shouldn't put my past experiences on you. You're right, not all men cheat." They gave each other a hug, and went to lunch. Kaz hoped she was right about Paul, she did not want to see Renee go through another bad relationship.

It was about 5:30pm. Renee had just made dinner and was feeding Anthony when Paul walked in.

"Can you braid my hair when you're done?" he asked. Paul had long hair down to his mid back. He was mixed with white and black so he had that good, easy hair to braid.

"Yeah let me get finished with them, and then I will start." Paul then walked off to take a shower.

Renee had just finished washing the kids up, and was starting to braid Paul's hair when there was a knock at the door. "Who is it?" she yelled. "It's me Adrian!" Adrian said from the other side.

"I thought he was coming earlier, it is almost 7 o'clock," said Paul.

"Well, that's what he told me." Renee said as she started to get up to answer the door.

"Hey" she said.

"Hey, this is Rob my cousin, he just rode along with me." Adrian said.

"Hey, Rob! Adrian, Rob, this is Paul. Paul this is Adrian and his cousin Rob." They all shook hands, and greeted one another. Adrian asked if it was ok to go to Jr.'s room, Renee said yes, and then he and Rob went to see Jr. Jr. was excited, Rob stayed for a little with Jr. and Adrian, then came back out with Renee and Paul. Renee felt the situation was so awkward.

She wanted to ask Adrian how he was, but Paul was there. Paul was making small talk with Rob, but looking at Jr.'s room out the corner of his eye. By the time Renee had finished Paul's hair, Adrian was making his way down the hall. "I can't believe how big he has gotten!" said Adrian.

"Yes, he is getting tall! Thank you so much for stopping by and giving him the games. I know that made his day." said Renee.

"Awe, that wasn't a problem, that's my homie." Adrian then looked over at Paul. Renee could tell he didn't care for him by Adrian's expression on his face. "Okay we out, ya'll take care," said Adrian and Rob. Then they were gone. Renee went back to see Jr's games and help him to bed. Jr. was so excited. "Look mommy, Adrian got me the new race game to play!" he said. "I see! That was so nice of him, but it's time to go to bed now though baby." Renee tucked him in, and checked on Anthony who was already sleeping in his crib, in her room. "Well, he doesn't' need to be coming by anymore," said Paul. "I am here now, Jr. has a father figure." Renee, didn't say a word, she felt Paul was jealous. Yes, Jr. liked Paul, but he enjoyed seeing Adrian, and Renee didn't want to take that from him. But Paul was her finance, the man she was going to marry. She needed to respect that. That was the last time Renee spoke to Adrian, or even took his calls.

Chapter 10
YOU ARE THE FATHER

"Well, I got the results back," said Renee. It had been a couple months now since she went ahead and filed for child support for Anthony. Of course, Kevin wanted a paternity test to make it linger out even longer. Altogether, it took almost four months for the results to come back 99.9%. He was the father.

"Girl, he knew he was the father, he was just delaying paying child support!" Kaz said.

"True, but now we have to go back to court for that. This is ridiculous. It's now September, Anthony will be one in another month!" Renee said as she shook her head.

Renee was feeling stressed taking care of two kids, and now Paul. Paul had lost his job once again, and was looking for work. Even though he was collecting unemployment, most of it went to mothers of his children, for child support. Light bills, phone bills, food, clothes, and gas for work. This was all weighing on her.

Renee had to give up her cell phone, which was just another extra bill she didn't need. Besides, she never went anywhere anyway besides work and home, and maybe here and there to see her parents. Even that had changed to once a month because she couldn't afford the gas. Renee had started to suspect Paul wasn't being so faithful either.

One day as she was getting out the car with the kids, she looked up to see her next-door neighbors staring at her out the windows. It was a mother and a daughter. The daughter looked to be around Renee's age with three kids. She was very skinny, and to Renee looked like she was on drugs. Renee never really spoke to them besides to say hi. This day was different. As Renee turned around to speak, she overheard the mother say, "She thinks she's the shit, and her man is sleeping with you when she's gone!" Renee pretended like she didn't hear her, and continued talking to Jr. She waved and went into her apartment. Jr.'s window was next to the window that they were sitting at. So, Renee put the kids in the kitchen, quietly walked to Jr.'s room, and closed the door so she could listen. "I know she heard me!" said the mother. "She heard you, she isn't going to say nothing to us, she ain't stupid. She need to worry about his ass with other women not just me!" The daughter said as they laughed. Then they changed the subject.

As she looked out Jr.'s window, she saw Paul's car pull up. As he seen her car, he turned back around and left. Renee knew then it was true. Renee was like clockwork. She came home from work the same time every day at 5:30pm. It was 2:38pm, and she had gotten off work early to take Anthony and Jr. for checkups. She didn't tell Paul.

She really wanted to see what he was doing all day while she was at work. Renee sat on the floor and began to cry. She couldn't believe what she had just heard and seen. Paul has been there daily, all day mostly, while Renee worked. It all made sense now. Lately, when they would return from somewhere, out the blue Paul would wave at them or say hi. He never used to do that. Renee always questioned it, but then thought he was just being nice. She went back out to the kids and made them lunch, then called Paul.

Ring, Ring, Ring. It was now 11:00 pm. Renee had been calling him since she saw him turn around. He never not picked up. She left messages and everything. "What was going on?" she thought. He had never done this before. Throughout the night, Renee called his phone, then called his mom. His mother had no clue where he was either. Renee had not mentioned the girl next door, she just left a message for him to call. She stayed up half the night worried, still no return call. The next morning around 10am, Renee's house phone rang.

"Hello," Renee answered. "Hey, it's me," said Paul.

Renee had so much anger and worry built up, she didn't even know how to begin.

"Before you even say anything, I don't remember what happened."

"All I know is I was arrested last night, and I been in jail all night. My sister posted bond, and I am at my mom's now," said Paul.

"What you mean you can't remember, and why did you come over here and turn around yesterday!" Renee was so angry.

"I had got a call for an interview, that's why I turned around," said Paul.

"That doesn't even make sense. You saw my car and turned around Paul. If that was the case, why didn't you call me then?" Renee started to yell.

She could tell that Paul had a hangover, he was slurring his words and everything.

"Can you just come pick me up please, then we can talk." He said.

"Pick you up? What the fuck? Where's your car at?" said Renee.

The phone was silent.
"It got repossessed last night after I was arrested." said Paul,

This entire story did not sound right to Renee, she knew the only way to get to the truth was to go to his mothers and pick him up.

"I will be there in about two hours, I have to get the kids ready," said Renee. She then hung up the phone.

The entire ride back from Paul's moms was silent. The kids were sleep, and Paul had told the entire story to Renee while they were at his mother's.

Basically, to make a long story short, he had gone out to the bar, upset because his child support order for his youngest child had been increased. Even though now he wasn't working, they based it on the final job he had. He had come home, but when he saw Renee's car, he couldn't tell her. While at the bar he got in a fight, picked up a bottle, and struck the guy in the head. The guy had to be escorted out by the ambulance, and they arrested him.

To Renee, it sounded like a bunch of lies he just made up. Turning around still does not make sense. Now he doesn't have a car, and they are down to only her vehicle for transportation. She was not about to tell **ANYONE** this story at all! There were already enough people telling her that he was wrong for her, she didn't need to give them another reason. Oh, and the girls next door, they just had a crush on him, as he stated. Paul begged for Renee to believe him, and she gave in and believed everything he said.

The next few weeks, Paul stayed home and claimed he was looking for work, as Renee worked. She was just getting by. Sometimes she would only have two dollars in her name till the next pay day.

She had started going to more than one food pantries now at local churches. She had probably hit every church in her area. That's how she kept food on the table. She had started looking for a better paying job.

Renee loved Howard University, but she needed more money. She landed an interview at a doctor's office in Laurel, Maryland. It wasn't far, about an hour and fifteen minutes, with traffic. She had called off work to go to the interview. The kids stayed home, Paul wasn't working so he could watch them till she came back.

"I will be back in probably an hour, wish me luck!" she told Paul as she was getting dressed.

Jr. and Anthony were in the living room watching cartoons. They were good kids, as long as they had a T.V and toys, they were fine.

"Ok, "Paul said as he was getting up.

Two hours had passed, and Renee pulled into the driveway. She had landed the job. She was going to be working in the front and back office as an office assistant with an outstanding Doctor. She was going to be starting a week after Anthony's birthday. That gave her plenty of time to give a two-week notice. She was excited! She was going to be making two dollars more, and that would really help.

As she unlocked the door to her apartment, Anthony was sitting on the couch crying as Paul was getting up and walking to the kitchen.

"Next time you go somewhere take him with you, he is a cry baby!" said Paul.

Renee went to pick Anthony up, "Why, what happened?" she asked. "He just cries for every little thing, you need to stop babying him so much!" said Paul. Anthony immediately stopped crying once she picked him up. He was a mama's boy, and that was just fine with her. She wasn't paying any attention to Paul, he was just upset he didn't have a job. Jr. was in his room sound asleep. Renee was so tired of Paul's temper tantrums. He would have them at least once a week feeling sorry for himself, then be back to normal the next day. The things he would say to Renee were totally inappropriate and unacceptable at times, but Renee stayed with him anyway. She believed that it was just a phase he was going through, and she could change him. Renee walked in the kitchen with Anthony in her arms, and turned to Paul.

"Paul, I got the job!" said Renee

"Good for you. Can I have the keys, I need to go down and get a paper?" he said. Paul took the keys, and left the apartment.

Renee was really getting irritated with Paul lately. She was feeding another mouth, and was getting tired of it. She believed if he really wanted a job, he would go to McDonalds, which was right down the street, and do what he had to do. She didn't know what to do about Paul, she loved him for one. She also didn't want to be alone again with two kids.

She didn't want to have to explain to people why she was single again. Things were getting better. She now was going to have a job paying more. The court date hearing was set for her child support for Anthony in November. Hopefully Paul would have a job by then, and they would be back on track.

The day had finally come. It was Oct 4, 2001, Anthony's birthday. Paul had landed a new job working nights at a warehouse part time. So, Renee, Jr., and Anthony were going to celebrate by themselves at home. It was the best time they ever had. Anthony had cake everywhere, and Jr. ate most of it. They took pictures, played, and laughed till late. Something was just different about that day to Renee. It was the first time in a long time she spent real quality time with her kids alone, and she liked it. She was proud of what she had accomplished so far, and where she was at. Besides their birth, that day was the best day she ever had in her life. Those were the times she cherished, just being a mother to her boys, and spending that quality time. Who knew that would all be taken away in a blink of an eye?

Chapter 11

LOSS

It was November 12, 2001, the first day at her new job. Her start date had gotten delayed. Luckily, Howard University worked with her and let her stay longer. She had left the kids with Paul since it was her first day, she wanted to be early. Paul was going to be home all day, and she could go straight to the job. As she was about to leave the house, she looked back at her bed, Anthony was sleep in the middle of the bed. Paul was on the other side of him. Renee had put Anthony in the bed with them last night late because he woke up crying, and she had to get up early. She knew if she just put him in the bed with them he would fall right to sleep. He did, but not without rubbing her braids first, as he liked to do.

"Hey, I'm leaving, I will call you around lunch time!" Renee whispered to Paul. Paul shook his head and rolled over.

Renee looked in Jr.'s room, he was spread out over his bed, asleep.

The ride to the new job wasn't bad, hardly no traffic, probably because she had left super early. Renee jumped right into work, and she loved it. It was now after 1 o'clock, she had never taken a lunch or break. She went to the back room to call home.

"Hello," said Paul.

"Hey, what's up? How's the kids, I've been so busy I-," Renee was cut off by Paul.

Paul was crying, "Anthony stopped breathing, they took him to the hospital!"

Renee just stared at the phone, "What do you mean? What? When? What time? Where is he?"

Paul began to tell Renee where he was taken. Renee immediately hung up the phone, and ran to get her keys.

"My son has been transferred to the ER, I have to go!" She screamed as she was getting her keys.

"Wait, do you want one of us to drive you?" asked a co-worker.

"No! I am OK, I just need to go!" Renee left. "Please God, let him be OK, please let him be OK!" She never really went to church at all since she had graduated school, and starting living on her own. But she knew, at that very moment she had to pray he was OK. It felt like an eternity before she got there, nearly 40 minutes later. As she barely parked, she ran inside the ER looking for anyone to help her. As she was walking in, she heard a voice say "Renee!" It was Kevin, Anthony's father.

"Where is Anthony?" she said.

"What you mean? He's here?" said Kevin. Kevin had no idea Anthony was in the hospital. He was at the ER with a friend who had injured himself.

Renee was looking for a doctor while talking to Kevin, who was walking right beside her confused.

"Hey, I'm looking for my son!" said Renee. "What's his name?" said the nurse. "Anthony Jackson." The nurse looked up at Renee. "Give me a moment. Can you please have a seat? I will find the doctor."

Renee and Kevin went into the room. As she began to tell him about her phone call to Paul, the doctor walked in.

"Hello, I am Doctor Jones, are you Renee?"

"Yes, where's my son?"

"And who is this?" asked the doctor; turning to Kevin.

"This is his father, he just happened to be here in the waiting room with someone else." said Renee.

"Oh, Wow," said Dr. Jones. "Where is my Son!" Renee started to raise her voice. "Ms. Jackson, I am sorry to tell you this, but your son has passed away." The doctor kept talking. Renee heard nothing else, and just started to cry. She felt like she was in a movie, and everything was happening slowly. In her head, the walls were caving in on her, and flashes of her son's face smiling kept going through her mind. This could not be true she thought, she looked over to Kevin who now had his arm wrapped around her, he was still talking to the doctor.

"Ms. Jackson, why did it take you so long to get here?" Renee could barely talk as she explained where she worked, and how she found out the baby even was there.

"Is there anyone you want to call?" said the doctor. Renee phoned her parents, she could only get out "Mom, Anthony is dead!" When she heard her mother scream, she passed the phone to the doctor. Renee was staring at the floor still in shock.

"I want to see my son!" she said. "Ok, Ms. Jackson. I do want to remind you he has tubes in him; they tried everything to save him," said the doctor. The doctor called a nurse to escort Renee and Kevin to the room. Kevin was silent. He held her hand as she walked, neither said a word.

As they turned the corner into the room, there were still EMT employees in the room and another nurse. There, in what looked like a gigantic bed, laid Anthony's lifeless body. He had tubes coming out of his nose and mouth, and he was laying on his back.

Renee began to cry, and make her way to the side of the bed. She leaned down and kissed him, and sat next to the bed while holding his hand. She looked over his entire body, and she kept thinking, maybe he fell from his crib. Anthony had fallen out of his bed two times before, and got right up like nothing happened.

"Did he have bruises? Did he fall? What happened?" she screamed out.

The staff looked at her, "We're sorry, we don't know what happened, he was unresponsive when we got to the house." said a nurse.

"Did your boyfriend tell you anything?" The Doctor asked while walking in.

"No, he just told me he stopped breathing!" Renee answered.

"Your finance is on the phone," a nurse came in with a phone as they were talking.

"No, he's gone!" said Renee. Paul didn't know what was going on. Since he was not the father the hospital would not update him.

"What happened?" Renee asked Paul. While everyone was waiting to hear the answer from Renee. Paul was on the other end telling her he had put them down for a nap, and went into to check on him and he was not breathing. Renee then hung up the phone. At that moment, she remembered Jr. was still at the house. She told the doctor what Paul had said. Kevin then told Renee she needed to go home.

Renee gave Anthony one last kiss, and walked out the room. The entire walk to the car she was still in a daze. Kevin was walking so fast she couldn't barely catch up with him. As she got up to his car, and was about to open the door, the doctor yelled for her.

"Hey, Renee! This is my card, and the card of a therapist here. If you need anything call me.

I understand he is trying to get you home, but to be his father, he doesn't seem as effected as you." said the doctor.

"He probably is not, he wasn't really never in his life." Renee said. The doctor then shook his head, and gave her a hug. Renee then turned around, and got in the car.

"Kaz, please go to my house!" Renee had called Kaz using Kevin's phone while in the car.

"What happened?!" Kaz said. Renee began to tell her about Anthony, Kaz screamed.

"Omg, I will meet you there." Said Kaz.

Renee was numb the entire ride to her apartment. Even though it was about 20 minutes from her house, it felt like an hour. The same hospital Anthony came into the world in, is the same one he left the world in. She didn't really say much to Kevin. She was still in shock, and in his own way, he was too. As they made their way up to the front door, Renee took a deep breath. How was she going to tell Jr.? She opened the door, and Jr came running to her. "Where is Anthony Mommy?"

Paul began to walk up to Renee, and put his arms around her. "I'm so sorry, I can't believe he's gone," he said. Renee couldn't hug him, she was still numb. Kevin informed Paul that Renee's car was at the hospital, and he would take him to pick it up.

They walked out the door. Kaz had just made it to the house before Renee did.

"Jr., Anthony is in heaven now with the angels," said Renee as she hugged him.

"Why mommy?" he asked.

"I don't know baby, I guess God wanted Anthony to be with him." Renee said as she began to cry.

Kaz put her arms around them both. Then Jr. out of the blue said, "Mommy, Paul was fake crying when he was on the phone with you." Renee and Kaz stared at each other.

"What do you mean fake crying, what is that?" asked Kaz.

"He had no tears coming out of his eyes, then when he hung up the phone, he was not crying."

Renee just kept quiet and said, "Ok, thank you. Can you go into your room and play for mommy?" Jr. began to go into his room.

"Renee, something does not feel right about all this. When I asked Paul, what happened, he said that Anthony was down for a nap. Something told him to go check on him, and when he did he was not breathing. Does he check on him any other time when he's asleep?" said Kaz.

"No, maybe he did because Anthony had fallen out the bed a couple weeks ago. I don't know, I am just so confused, my baby is dead!" said Renee and she burst into tears. Kaz stayed with Renee until her Mom, Dad, and sister showed up. Everyone was at a loss for words, no one knew what to say.

This had never happened in the family. Taylor went to Jr's room to keep him busy.

"What did I do wrong?" Renee said sitting on her bed. Her father and mother were by her side. "You didn't do nothing wrong, Renee, this is not your fault," her mother said and put her arm around her. Renee's father turned around and went downstairs to talk to Kevin alone. That was not going to be a good talk, Renee thought, while her mother stayed with her consoling her. Paul was in the living room, sitting with his hands on his head. After a while of talking to her family, Raymond and Ann started to head back home. Taylor stayed with Renee for the rest of the night, she was going to take them to Gettysburg in the morning.

That night as everyone went to bed, Taylor slept with Jr., and Renee sat in her room with Paul. She asked him again what had happened.

"We got up, and I made blueberry pancakes for them. Anthony ate all of his food, and so did Jr. I then turned on the TV, and they watched cartoons. Then later, they went down for a nap. Something told me to go check on him, and when I did, I noticed he wasn't breathing. I then called 911." Said Paul.

Renee just sat quietly, and then her and Paul began to hug. She was so distraught over the entire situation. They were sitting on her bed in the bedroom. Every time she looked at Anthony's crib she began to cry.

"I can't sleep in here," she said. "I'm going to sleep in the living room, it hurts to much in here." Paul followed her to the living room.

Renee laid on the love seat while crying herself to sleep. Paul was on the couch, asleep. It had to be about midnight or later when Paul suddenly got up, and walked past Renee. Renee jumped up in the middle of her sleep, and started breathing heavy. She looked at Paul, and started to have chills go down her back. Something was off, she didn't know what it was, but something just did not feel right. She didn't know why, maybe it was because he walked by so quickly. When she turned to look to see where he was going, he was entering the restroom. As she laid back down, her heart was still beating very fast.

That night she slept maybe two hours, then she just laid there, staring at the ceiling, thinking of her baby. He was such a good baby. "Why has God done this to me? What did I do to deserve this?" she thought to herself. "He's not gone, he can't be, this is a dream. I just need to wake up!" But she was awake, this was not a dream at all.

It was about 9:00 am the next morning, and everyone was getting dressed for the drive to Gettysburg. Taylor was driving, but first they had to drop Paul off at his moms. It was going to be a long day. The phone began to rang.

"Hello," said Taylor. "Yes, she is. May I ask who is calling?"

"Ok, hold on. It's a detective," said Taylor, as she handed Renee the phone.

"Hello, this is Renee."

"This is Detective Green, I'm sorry to hear about your loss. I was calling to see if you and your boyfriend can stop by the Prince Georges Police department for some questioning?"

"Yes, what time do you want us to come?" said Renee.

"Whenever you can, we will be here all day."

"Ok, give me about an hour," said Renee.

"Sounds great, we will see you then." He said.

Renee hung up the phone, while turning around to face her sister and Paul.

"He wants us to come down to the police station for requesting." Renee said.

"For what?" said Paul. Renee watched enough TV to know that anytime there is a death in a home, especially of an infant child, they must investigate.

"For Anthony, they want to ask questions."

"Ok, when do we have to go?" asked Paul.

"I told him we will be there in an hour. Let's just get our stuff together and go," said Renee.

She started packing clothes for her and Jr. As she was in her room, she kept stopping and staring at Anthony's crib.

She then walked over to his crib and looked around. It was not in the same spot it was this morning.

The crib was by the window. She had moved it a week ago, because it was getting cold, next to the door. Now it was back against the window. She then looked at the walls to see if anything was different. She didn't know why she was looking, she just stared at everything. She then looked down into the crib. All the sheets were gone, and so were Anthony's teddy bears.

"Paul, come here!" she said.
"Where is the sheets on his bed, and teddy bears?"

"The police took all that yesterday when they came." said Paul.

"Why? And why is his bed over here?" "I don't know why, they just took it. I had moved the bed over to the window when he went to sleep so he couldn't hear the TV as good from the living room." He said.

Renee shook her head ok, and they began to walk out to the living room. Everyone made their way to the car, and headed for police station. Upon arrival at the police station, Taylor took Jr. to the park, while Renee and Paul went into the police station.

When they entered the police station, Mr. Green was waiting. He took Renee to one room, while Paul was taken to another room.

Mr. Green went over the procedures when there is a death at home, and why they were asking questions. He started asking Renee what happened from the time she woke up till she got to the hospital. Renee was so upset, she had to rehash the worst day of her life again. She told the detective everything once again. He asked the same questions repeatedly. She was so angry, why does he keep asking me the same questions, she said to herself. After asking her the same question for what seem to be like forever, Mr. Green stood up and walked out. Renee just sat, closed her eyes, and began to cry again.

"Ok, Ms. Jackson I think we are done here. I just need to take a picture of you." He said. "Wait!" said Renee. "What happened to my baby? I need to know!" said Renee.

"Ms. Jackson, what I am about to tell you, you cannot tell your boyfriend or anyone else." He said.

Renee sat back, her heart started to beat fast again, just like the night before when Paul walked by her." I won't, what is going on?"

"We're not sure, and I shouldn't even be telling you this but, we believe your child was hurt by your boyfriend." said the detective. "What!" Renee screamed. "Shooooo! I am sorry Ms. Jackson, but we won't be sure until the autopsy is back. But how your son came in, he didn't just pass away." he said.

"From what we can see, he does have injuries associated with abuse."

Renee began to cry, she wanted to get out the room, and go to Paul. She didn't know what she was going to do to him. Mr. Green continued to explain to Renee she could not tell Paul. That would ruin the entire investigation.

"How can I not say anything, I have to leave here with him" she said.

"I know Ms. Jackson, but you must not say anything or even let him think we're on to him. Honestly this is all circumstantial evidence at this time."

"He could never do that, he loves my kids like they're his own. Anthony fell out his bed a couple of weeks ago, and maybe he hurt himself. I didn't know." said Renee.

"He could have, but we don't think this is something from a couple weeks ago. Whatever happened to your son happened that day. Now we could be wrong, but we won't know for sure, until then." Mr. Green repeated to Renee that they would not know everything that took place for sure, until the autopsy comes back. She had to be strong and be herself around him. An autopsy could take several weeks to several months. Mr. Green then walked Renee out to the picture area, and took her picture. Renee was in such a trans from the new information, she walked for what felt like hours back out in the waiting area, where Taylor was sitting waiting for her.

It was now almost noon, Renee had been back in that room for about an hour and a half.

"Mom came and got Jr., what happened?" Taylor asked. "Nothing, they just wanted to ask me about what happened yesterday. They're doing an investigation." Renee then looked over past Taylor, "Where is Paul?" Renee said. "He didn't come out yet," said Taylor "Don't worry. They do investigations all the time when it comes to babies. They are just trying to figure out what happened." said Taylor.

Renee wanted to tell Taylor so bad what the detective said, but she kept it in. She knew if she told anyone, they would automatically think he did it. Renee honestly believed the detective was wrong. In her mind, Anthony had passed away. She didn't know why and how, but she believed her fiancé didn't have nothing to do with it.

As Taylor and Renee sat in the waiting area, it felt like time was going so slow. Then, finally four hours after they had originally got there, she looked up and saw Paul walking towards them.

"Hey, you guys ready?" Paul said as he ran his hands through his hair.

"What took so long? You've been back there for a little over four hours." said Renee.

"I don't know, they just kept asking me questions over and over about the same thing. I told them the same story over and over. I don't know, but let's get out of here." said Paul.

They grabbed their jackets, and began to walk out. As they approached the front door, Renee looked back, and Mr. Green was standing in the doorway. They made eye contact, then they both turned around, and walked away. Renee could still hear his words in her head, it wouldn't go away.

"WHATEVER HAPPENED TO YOUR SON, HAPPENED THAT DAY."

Chapter 12
STAGES OF GRIEF

It had been a little over a week since Anthony's death. Renee and her parents had decided for a cemetery closed casket funeral in a couple of days. She woke up thinking about Anthony, and went to sleep thinking about him. Days were so hard for her. Her family and friends were all around her. She wouldn't take any calls from anyone, she didn't want to hear nothing. No one knew how she felt, and there are no words they could say to help her. She was angry. She was angry that she left the kids at home that day. She started blaming herself. She still didn't fully believe that Paul had anything to do with it. But then the words of the detective would always come back.

She was angry at God; how could he take her son? She started to tell herself there wasn't a God. How could a God that is so loving, patient, and kind take a baby so young? He had all his life to live. Renee would only eat one meal a day, if that. She laid in bed the majority of the day, crying on and off. One day, she was in bed thinking about Anthony, and her anger with God. She was screaming in her mind to God, "How could you do this to me? Was it because I had an abortion? What kind of God are you?" Renee heard a voice yell out.

"RENEE!"

She quickly rose and looked around, no one was there. Everyone had left the house, she was alone. The voice was loud, and whoever said it, said it in an angry way. She thought, "What was that?" She laid back down, and began thinking how angry she was at God again. What kind of God takes a child from his mother? What kind of God puts this much sadness on a person? There is no GOD! That's how she felt, and no one could tell her any different now. Her family would come over and pray over her, she just listened and kept her mouth shut. She had it in her mind that they can pray all they want, to a God that doesn't exist.

A couple hours later, her family had returned, and Jr. entered the room. "Mommy, I had a dream last night about Anthony!" he said. Renee sat up in the bed and motioned for Jr. to come to her. As he sat beside her, he started to tell her the story.

"We were at our house, and God had me on his lap. When I looked down, Anthony was on the floor playing with a toy. I then got down and started playing with him. We played for a while, then God said he had to take Anthony with him." said Jr.

Renee started to tear up, as she listed to him. "I told God, I didn't want him to take Anthony, but he said he had to, but I would see him again" said Jr.

"Then he picked Anthony up, Anthony gave me a kiss, then they disappeared."

This made Renee feel good that Jr. could still see his brother in his dreams. "Aww Jr, that was nice of God to let you see Anthony. Was Anthony ok?" asked Renee.

"He was fine. He was smiling and playing," said Jr.

"What did God look like, and how do you know it was God?" said Renee.

"He was dark-skinned, and his hair was cut low. He told me he was God mommy." said Jr. Something told Renee deep inside, that he really did see this. She was always told that children can see stuff that adults can't. She never really told Jr. about God or Jesus, so she knew this wasn't just his imagination. But, she still felt the same way about God. This didn't change her feelings. She was just happy Jr. had some comfort.

"Jr., can you tell me again what happened the day Anthony got sick," she said. "Yes, me and Anthony ate blueberry pancakes that morning. Then we played and watched T.V. Then we went down for a nap. When I woke up, Anthony was gone mommy."

"Where did Paul say Anthony was when you asked him?" said Renee.

"He said the doctor came and took him to the hospital because he was sick. Then you called and he started fake crying," said Jr. That statement still brought Renee to chills.

"Fake crying."

"But, when he was on the phone, he said he had to find a way to get rid of you." Said Jr.

Renee, looked at Jr. "Wait what phone call Jr?"

"When he told me to lay down for a nap, he was talking to someone on the phone. I heard him say, 'I have to get rid of Renee first!' I don't know what he said after that because he must of walked away from my door."

This had to be true, Renee thought. This was a six-year-old boy. He was not going to make this up. Hell, he didn't know how to lie at that age!

"Where was Anthony when you went to sleep?"

"He had already gone to sleep. Paul had put him in his crib. When I was walking to my room, I looked in your room, and he was asleep in the crib." said Jr.

"Jr, where was the crib in my room?"

"It was by the window." said Jr.

Renee thought, to herself. That's not where she left it that morning. Renee began to hug Jr. She thought to herself, well, at least Jr. got to spend some more time with him, even though he said God showed him. Renee then thought, even though God took my other baby, he was giving Jr. comfort. This does not make sense, she thought.

It was the day before Anthony's homecoming, and the funeral home had just called. They said that the family could come down and see him. This was only for Renee's immediate family. All her sisters', including Desiree who had flew in from California. Renee, all her sisters', and mom and dad entered the funeral home. Her brother, younger sister and Jr. did not attend. This would be too much for them. As they walked down, Renee saw a little white casket. As she got closer, she saw Anthony's little body dressed in the clothes she had picked out for him. He looked so at peace. She put one finger in his hand. She felt his hand squeeze around her finger and she began to cry. "Why God, why?" she cried out to herself. She could hear her sisters and mother behind her crying. As her dad stood beside her, he whispered to her.

"You know this isn't Anthony, this is just his body. His spirit is in heaven right now." He said. Little did he know, that was not helping because Renee was blaming God now. She was angry all over again that he took her baby. She just nodded her head, she couldn't move. She stared at Anthony. She looked him up and down repeatedly, from his head to his shoes.

"Where's his shoes?" she said. The funeral owner came up to the casket. "We were unable to put shoes, on him. He said. Renee shook her head, and began to cry again.

They had been at the funeral home for a while when her father motioned it was time to leave. Renee didn't want to go. She felt if she stayed with him, he would wake up. But she knew, deep down, that was not going to happen. As she kissed Anthony good-bye, she laid a picture of him and Jr. together in his casket. It was a picture that they had took together a couple weeks before Anthony's death. She also added a teddy bear too. Since the police had took his teddy bear in his crib, she picked another one he played with. She was numb for the rest of the day. She laid in bed that night saying to herself…

"My baby is gone, I might as well let myself leave too. If I die, I will be with him, and all will be fine."

It was the next morning, and it was the day of the graveside funeral. Renee was helping Jr. get dressed when she heard Paul enter the house. She hadn't really spoken to him, but maybe two times since they left the police station. He came into the bedroom where she was.

"Hey Jr., how are you?" he said. "Hi," Jr. said, as he walked out into the kitchen where the rest of the family was. "How are you?" Paul asked Renee.

"Ok, I guess. I don't know how I am supposed to be."

"I miss you. I've been crying day and night. I miss him too." said Paul.

They hugged, and then walked out where everyone else was to get ready to leave. Paul had drove Renee's car with her sisters in it, and Renee road with her parents and Jr. to the funeral.

When they got to the cemetery, there was a lot of people there. All of Renee's family and friends, even Renee's work friends from DC were there. She didn't see Anthony's father. She hadn't spoken to him since that day at the hospital. She knew he had to know about the funeral because they had mutual friends.

Renee's uncle gave the eulogy over Anthony. Renee stood there trying to listen to what he was saying, but she couldn't. She just stared at the casket thinking about her baby. She had written a poem for Anthony that was going to be read during the funeral. As another uncle began to sing, she looked to her right, Paul was standing right beside her looking at the ground. She just began to stare at him. She looked at his face, and couldn't stop looking at him. The words, *"Whatever happened to your son happened that day,"* came back. Paul then looked over at Renee, kissed her on the cheek, and said "I'm sorry."

"What was he saying sorry for?" thought Renee. She looked down at her hand, and handed the poem to her sister to read out loud.

To my son Anthony,

Mommy's little baby. That's what I called you. You came into my life and left so soon. Although I am sad and hurt at this time, the only thing that keeps me going is your big brother, and remembering all our happy times. In closing, my son, all I can say is you will be missed and loved every day and in every way. P.S. Now, you will always be mommy's little baby angel. Love Mama.

This letter was all so true. What Renee's family didn't know is, while she was home, she was also thinking of ways to take her life. Towards the end of the service, Anthony's dad walked up, and put a flower wreath beside the casket. Renee was happy he had come to say good bye to his son, but also angry. She hadn't heard nothing from him at all. She thought, he could have at least called to see how she was.

The funeral was over, and Renee had just sat back in her dad's car when some of her friends came up to give her a hug. As they walked away, Kevin came up to the car with his mother. He handed Renee an envelope, and his mother began to hug her. Anthony favored Kevin's mother so much, she had never gotten the chance to see him. It was all Kevin's fault! If he had of never denied him and manned up, she would've been able to spend time with Anthony.

After the funeral, everyone went to the local church and ate. All of Renee's friends and family were there. People from DC, Maryland, and most of her friends and family from Gettysburg. She felt so loved by everyone. She was happy to see everyone, but not under these conditions. She tried not to talk about Anthony's death to anyone. She knew people had questions, hell so did she, but this was not the time. Paul was mingling with people, while Renee stayed seated and spoke to friends. Kevin and his family did not attend the repass, she didn't really care. She wanted this day to be over and done.

Dear Diary,

I buried my baby today, I buried my baby today, I BURIED MY BABY TODAY, AND ITS ALL YOUR FAULT GOD! You took my child, even if the detective says it was Paul! You let it happen. YOU, YOU! Now what am I supposed to do? Be happy, get over it, NO! I can't! I want to die. I want to be with my baby, I want to lay next to him in that coffin! My baby is alone, in the ground, covered in dirt. He might be crying for me, his MOMMY! I can't help him unless I die too! How do I do it? When do I do it? I don't know, but I will have to do it soon. I can't wait too long. Mommy's coming Anthony.

For the next couple of weeks, Renee went to the cemetery daily. She felt she needed to go daily, to be with Anthony. Jr. had been enrolled in school, and he was coping. He still did not quite grasp the entire situation, but at that age what kid does. He continued to have dreams every now and then, with him and his brother. When Renee was about to go to the cemetery, her dad asked if he could go. "Yeah, Dad, it's Ok!" said Renee. As Renee was riding with her dad, he started to talk about Anthony.

"Renee, I can't imagine what you're going through. I know how I was when my mother passed. People say the death of your mother or child is the worst." He said "I see you go to the cemetery every day. You know he is not in that grave, right?" he said. "I know he physically isn't, but I just feel I need to be there daily." Renee said. "I can understand that, but you can talk to Anthony anytime and anywhere, he will hear you. Something I never told no one is when my mother died, I wanted to take my life." Her father said. "My mom was the only person I could talk to. I could tell her anything. She always told me to pray about my problems, and everything would be ok. There is not a day that goes by that I don't think about her. I knew I couldn't take my life because she wouldn't have wanted that, and I have my kids to think about. You have another son that you need to be here for."

Renee thought, how did he know I was having those suicidal thoughts? She hadn't told anyone about them, but for some reason her Dad was confirming her thoughts.

"Sometimes you can love something too much," he said. Renee was confused. What did he mean, she didn't love her other child? "And you lose focus of what's around you." He finished.

"What I mean by that is, sometimes love is about letting go." He said. "Not saying you should let go and never think about Anthony again. But you must let him go in peace, knowing that his spirit will always be with you." Renee's father turned and looked at her, "Jr. needs you."

Renee was silent, what he said made sense. She did have to let him go, but she didn't know how, and she wasn't ready to. She knew Anthony would always be with her, but didn't know how to let go of him. She knew she had to be strong for Jr., he needed her too. She felt like she wasn't as close to Jr. than she was before Anthony was born. Mainly because Anthony was a baby, and she was always making sure he was safe. She spent time with both, but Anthony did get a lot more attention because he was smaller.

Now her and Jr. were building an even closer bond together. All they had was each other. She couldn't leave this world, and leave Jr. behind.

That was her first born, she loved him and Anthony, and would give her life for both. She had to stay strong for Jr. He needed her, she couldn't leave him. But, in her mind she was leaving Anthony alone too, he was in the grave alone.....

Renee and Raymond visited the cemetery, and then went to get lunch and started home. They talked about a lot of things. Raymond tried to keep the conversation off Anthony, and on to other topics. They talked about family, Raymond's job, and his parents. After lunch, they had a couple of other stops that he had to make, and then they picked up Jr. from school.

When she had gotten home, her mother said the detective had phoned, and wanted her to come back down to the police station tomorrow.

"For what?" Renee asked. "He said he had a couple more questions." said Renee's mother. Renee then pulled her mother and father in the living room, while her brother kept her son busy.

"I need to tell you all what the detective told me last time I was there." Renee said. She proceeded to tell them what the detective told her. Her parents were silent. "I don't know, I just can't see Paul doing anything to that boy, are they sure?" said Raymond. "You never know what someone might do. I can't see it either, but if there is evidence that he did," said her mother. "Renee, what do think?"

"I just can't see it either. I keep thinking maybe they got it wrong, but the stuff Jr. has told me. Then, with the detective saying it had to happen that day. What am I supposed to think? It's been very hard to keep this inside. I want to ask Paul so bad, but the detective told me not to let him know they're investigating him."

"Well, I am going with you tomorrow, you never know what those police will try to do. They might turn it on you, I don't trust police!" said Raymond.

The next day, Renee and Raymond drove to the police department. Renee was in the same room with the same detective. He went over all the same questions he asked before, then he walked out and left Renee in the room alone. When Renee looked down at the side table, she saw a folder with a picture half hanging out. The folder had Anthony's name on it. She started to look at the picture closer. She could not make out the picture. The only thing she could see was something that looked like a bruise, but couldn't see where it was.

What Renee didn't know was, while she was in the room, the detective had gone back out to the front for some paperwork, and Renee's father was sitting there. He had become angry his daughter had been back there for almost an hour and a half. "Hey, how much longer you going to have my daughter back there!" Raymond asked him.

"And you are, sir?" the detective asked. "I am her father, I want to know what's going on." Raymond was not loud, but upset about Renee.

"Well, we asked your daughter to come down, not you. We don't know how long she will be here," said the detective in a demanding voice.

"Look here man, that's my daughter. If you have a daughter, you would feel the same way! Ya'll take her back there for this long, and you can't tell me when she's coming out! Do I need to get a lawyer? I need to know what's going on!" Raymond began to raise his voice. At that time the detective realized that Raymond was getting upset.

"Mr. Jackson, I am sorry. You're right, I would feel the same way. I will have your daughter out of here soon. You don't need a lawyer, she will be free to go."

"Okay, thank you! That's all I wanted to know." said Raymond as he sat back down.

Right when Renee was about to pick up the folder, the detective walked back in. Renee immediately became angry. She was tired of getting the run around.

"What is going on? You told me to keep quiet about Paul, and still nothing has happened!" she began to scream.

"I know Renee, we can't bring him in without the complete autopsy report. This could take weeks to get. I am sorry I have to put you in this position, but we have to make sure the evidence is complete. I will call you, and keep you updated on everything." he said.

"Yes, but I still must keep quiet, this is hard to do!" Renee started to cry again. Then the detective walked her back out to her father.

Christmas and the New Year came and went. Renee had just moved into a two-bedroom apartment about eight miles from her parents. She had also starting working in the office at the local hospital. She hadn't heard back from the detective since the day before Christmas. She had phoned him to ask about the investigation, but still the same thing, no final report yet. Renee was still talking to Paul almost three times a week. She had told him after the funeral she needed her space, and he understood.

"Hello!" said Renee as she answered her home phone. "Hey Renee, it's me Paul. I miss you so much!" Renee didn't know what to say, she was silent. "Hey, how are you?" she said. "I have been ok. I started working, so I have a job now. I've been thinking a lot about you and Anthony. I was laying downstairs last night on the couch. My nephew had left his toys at my mom's, and they were on the floor.

I was just dozing off, and one of his trucks turned on by its self. The lights and everything just started flashing, and it drove across the room. I knew it was Anthony playing with it. It scared me at first, then I just thought, he's playing."

Renee became angry. It had been almost four months since Anthony's death, and she hadn't had a dream about him yet. Why is that? Her son had one, even another family member, now Paul.

"Yes, he probably was playing," said Renee sadly. Paul talked for a little while longer telling Renee about a dream he had too. He said that he was in a field by himself, and Anthony came out of nowhere. He picked him up, hugged him, and told him he was sorry. He then stated, Anthony told him he forgives him.

Renee immediately reacted, "Why are you saying sorry to him? And why did you say sorry to me at the funeral? What are you sorry about? Did you do something?" It just came out. Renee couldn't take the words back. She was about to tell him what the police was saying, but then Paul said;

"I blame myself for his death, I was watching him. Maybe if I would have checked on him sooner, I could have saved him." He then began to cry. Renee reassured him that there was nothing that he could have done, it was his time she said. They talked for a little longer.

Paul kept asking Renee if he could come up for the weekend? He was going to have a four-day weekend, and her birthday was coming up. Renee told him he could come that Friday and they hung up.

In her mind, she wanted to keep him close. She felt if he had any clue the police are on to him, he might flee. As she hung up she began to cramp. She had been having cramps on and off since Anthony's death. She still was not sleeping some nights, depressed, and was still having suicidal thoughts at times. She decided it was time to go to the doctor.

PTSD-Post Traumatic Stress Disorder. That's what she was diagnosed with. The doctor put her on Paxil daily, and gave her some material for grief support. Renee didn't want to go to a support group. She had now taken up smoking, and that was the support for her. She started smoking almost a pack a day. It relaxed her, and eased her mind from wondering. She had also completed STD testing while she was there too. She didn't think she had anything, she had been with the same person for over a year.

It was Friday. Renee had picked Paul up from the bus station at noon. She was off from work that day, so her and Paul went to the cemetery, then back to the apartment.

They waited for Jr. to come home from school then ordered pizza. Jr. was ok with Paul around, he wasn't extremely happy, but he didn't seem like he hated him or anything. Renee kept watching to see if Jr. would say anything about Paul, but he didn't. She had promised herself a little after the funeral, she would stop asking Jr. questions about that day. He was already young, and she knew this would always affect him, as it would her.

That night, Jr. slept in his room, as Renee and Paul slept in Renee's room. Paul slept on his side of the bed, and she on hers. In no way, did she want him to think they were together, or getting back together. She was keeping him at bay, while waiting for the autopsy.

Saturday morning had come. Renee opened her eyes, and Paul was looking at her.
"Dang, why you all in my face!" she said. "Do you remember last night?" he said. "What do you mean?" Renee asked as she was getting out the bed. "In the middle of the night, you sat up in the bed and looked over at me. When I looked at you, Anthony's face was like a glow over yours. Then I went to kiss you, and you laid back down." he said. Renee felt a chill come over her body. The same chill she had that night Anthony died, and Paul walked passed her in the middle of the night. "Wow, I don't remember that!" she said. She went to restroom to freshen up, and get dressed. Just then, the phone rang.

"Hello!" she said as she answered the phone. "Hello is this Renee Jackson?" a lady on the other end asked. "Yes, this is." said Renee. "This is Marie from Dr. Lee's office, we got your results back. You have tested positive for two STD's." She said.

Renee was tongue tied, "What? But I don't have symptoms, how is this possible?" The nurse started to explain to Renee. "These are both curable sexually transmitted diseases. You were negative for everything else, including HIV. We can treat these two STD's, and in about two weeks they will be gone."

Renee felt relief, but still angry. She made arrangements to pick up her antibiotic. She now knew that Paul was not being faithful, and it all was out now. He could not lie his way around this. If she had this he had it too. She also had got checked out right after Anthony's birth, and had nothing. She and Paul had stopped using condoms once they became engaged. Renee was on birth control, and this was the man she was going to marry. Well, so she thought.

Renee got off the phone, and sent Paul to the store to get some bread. She quickly got on the phone and called her cousin Van. She was in the medical field, and could tell her more about the STD. "Renee, it is curable and you will be fine, but you need to get him out of that house." She said. Renee then began to tell Van about what Paul said he saw last night.

"Girl, that's just God giving you confirmation. You don't need that autopsy. He definitely had something to do with Anthony's death. I felt it at the funeral, that something was not right."

"I just can't believe this, I'm going to get Jr. stuff ready to take him to my parents. Then I will take Paul to the bus station."

"Okay, but Renee, as much as I know you want to confront him about Anthony you can't! You don't know what he might do if he knows that they suspect him. Just tell him about the STD's, and that's the reason why you want him out." Before Renee could answer, Paul was coming back through the door. She quickly hung up the phone.

"I need to talk to you right now!" she looked at him, and turned to walk to her room.

"Jr., get dressed. You're going to go to Grandma's and Pop." She said. Renee closed the door, and proceeded to tell Paul about the call from the nurse.

"How could you do this to me? You been sleeping with people the entire time, haven't you?" she said. "No. I mean, remember the night when I got arrested?" he said. "Yes!" she said. "I was at the strip club, I was confused, I had no job, I was depressed, and I wanted to have some fun. I don't remember what fully happened, but it did end in me getting in a fight at the strip club that night."

"You mean to tell me you slept with someone, and you don't remember!" she screamed.

"Yes, I guess I did" said Paul. "That is the dumbest thing I ever heard, it doesn't matter now. You gave me two STD'S. Luckily, they're both curable. But what if I had of gotten AIDs or something? You got to go, we can never be together Paul. Get your stuff together, I am going to drop Jr. off and I'm taking you to the bus station!"

Renee walked out of the room without giving Paul any other chance to talk. She was in Jr.'s room helping him get ready, when out of the corner of her eye, she saw Paul pacing back and forth in the hallway. She then began to get the chills again, and started to get scared. What was he going to do? It was only her and Jr. in the house, she started to walk to the front door.

"Come on let's go!" she yelled to Paul.

Paul walked out of the bedroom with a look on his face that Renee had never seen before. He didn't look mad, he just looked different, she couldn't explain it.

She was seeing him really for the first time. This was not the man she fell in love with at all.

As they approached the bus station, Paul turned to Renee.

"I am sorry, I want us to be together, please, I need you." he said.

Renee remembered what her cousin had said, about not letting Paul know about the investigation.

"Paul, I am not in the mood to talk about us.

You can call me whenever you want," she said.

They arrived at the bus station, and Paul got out of the car. "I love you Renee," he said. Renee looked at him, and closed the door. She knew if he called she was not going to answer. She was done. That was the last time she spoke to Paul.

Chapter 13
NEW LIFE

Months had passed since Anthony's death. Renee was still smoking a pack of cigarettes a day, and taking her Paxil. She was working full-time, and still going out to the grave at least once a week now. She was still blaming herself for what happened to Anthony. She still felt that if they had gone to daycare, her baby would be alive.

Her routine now was work, pick up Jr. from school, help him with homework, cook dinner, then bed. She played with him as much as she could. After he would go to bed, she would sneak out back every night for her last cigarette of the night. She would look up at the stars, and think of Anthony. What was he doing? Who was he with? She stayed up most nights reliving that day, in her head.

The one thing that had bothered her though, was that she hadn't cried in a long time. She sat trying to remember the last time she cried. Usually when she thought of Anthony, tears came flowing, but not anymore. It was like her emotions were cut off. Before she was put on the meds, when Jr. would cry, she would too. Her heart would break when she saw him cry. But now, she had no emotions. Even when Jr. would cry, she hugged him, and told him everything would be Ok.

Jr. was still telling her about his dreams here and there, playing with his brother. She hadn't had one dream at all about Anthony. She still blamed God. "First you take my child, then you don't let me see him again, at all!" Everyone else around her thought she was slowly getting better because she was working, and becoming a little more active, but she wasn't. Renee was slowly going deeper and deeper into depression.

"Well, at least I can't feel the pain anymore." she said to herself. She couldn't. She couldn't feel the pain she was feeling laying in the bed at her parents daily, when Anthony first died. She could think of everything, but no emotions. It was just thoughts.

Renee walked around to the mailbox and walked back into her apartment. While going through the mail, she saw an envelope from the examiner's office. As she opened it, she wondered what it was. What could she possibly be getting from the examiner's office? Then she realized, there was only one thing that could be coming from there. It was Anthony's death certificate. As she scanned down the certificate, she got down to cause of death.

"**MULTIPLE BLUNT FORCE TRAUMA, DEATH RULED HOMICIDE!**" she read out loud. Renee let the paper slide through her hand, and onto the floor. She stared at the wall with no expression.

She knew without a doubt that Paul had caused the death of her child. She grabbed her cigarettes, and went back outside. She screamed, no tears would fall. She threw rocks as far as she could to release her anger, no tears. She then screamed up to God, "WHYYYY!" She ran back in the house and grabbed a beer out the refrigerator. She then made her way back up to the porch, and lit another cigarette. She smoked, and drank until her pack of cigarettes was almost empty, and she had run out of beer. She started thinking to herself again "I want to cry, why can't I cry?" As she closed her cigarette case, she thought, "Now I know the truth."

Renee went day by day with the same routine. It was getting worse. She was cutting off contact with people. She would not return calls, and she would keep to herself. She laid in bed nightly, and would not fall to sleep, just stare at the walls. She started calling off work, and just staying in her room while Jr. was at school. She would rock back and forth thinking of ways to hurt Paul. "I want to kill him just like he killed my child!"

Renee's family didn't know the depth of how bad she was getting. She put on a good front when her parents came by. She would make sure the place was tidy, and her cigarettes where not in sight.

It was a Sunday evening, Renee had just put Jr. to bed, and walked on the back porch for her nightly routine, cigarettes and a beer. Renee slowly made her way back in the house, she was dizzy and staggering from side to side. It was nearly midnight now, Renee passed out for a couple hours, then woke up. She was laying in her bed going through channels, when she came across a church station. The T.V. said Joyce Meyer. She didn't know who that was. She sat and listened to her preach. The program was almost over. Renee started reliving everything again in her head. Flashes of the hospital, Anthony lying in the bed, coffin, remembering his smile was all coming to her at once. She had flashes of the good times with Paul and the kids, them all laughing together, then flashes of her past relationships and abuse. The lady started talking about being saved, giving your life to God. Renee sat up in the bed, and really started listening, "God hears you in your time of need, he will never leave you. Confess with your mouth." Renee slowly started getting out the bed, she made her way to the head of her bed, and got on her knees.

"HELP ME! I am so sorry for blaming you...Lord, I ask you to come into my life. I believe your son Jesus Christ died for my sins. Lord I asked you to forgive me for all my sins. I am a sinner and I want to be saved, show me the way to be with you.

I thank you Lord for my life, I thank you for my family, friends, my son, Lord I ask you to hold me, and stay in my life, show me right from wrong, help me Lord! I need you please, please, please, please, take me out of this dark place, please, please... ... ...

Renee prayed like never before. She asked God to release her pain. Suddenly, Renee started talking in tongues, she didn't know what was going on. She had heard people when she was younger talking like this, but didn't know what it was. As she was on her knees, she saw herself on her knees praying. It was like her body rose above her, then she fell back into it. This went on for what seemed like hours. When Renee was finished, she had tears, real tears coming out her eyes. She slowly made her way back into the bed, and continued to praise him. She felt a tingle from her head to her toes. For the first time since Anthony's death, she slept all night with no interruptions.

The next morning Renee woke up early, she felt different. She didn't feel like she had no emotions anymore, she felt like a new woman. She didn't know what really happened to her last night. She knew she had cried out to God for salvation, but something else had happened. She looked to her bedside table, and reached for her Paxil she took every morning. She picked up the bottle, and just stared at it, "I don't need this anymore." she said.

She got up, went to the bathroom, and poured the medication down the toilet. She began to brush her teeth, and she washed her face. She had this glow. Her face had broken out so badly after Anthony's death, but today it was clear. She still had the black spots from old acne scars, but her face was smooth. She stared in the mirror, and just smiled at herself.

"Mom, can I come in?" Jr. asked from the outside of the bathroom door. "Yes, baby good morning!" Renee had the biggest smile ever. "Mom, why are you so happy? You never smile that much." said Jr. "This is a new day baby, a new day." Renee reached over and gave him a kiss. They got ready, and out the door they went.

When Renee had dropped Jr. off at school, she looked over into her purse for cash to get a coffee. As she was going through her purse, she noticed her cigarette case. She hadn't had a cigarette this morning. She was like clockwork, she needed that first smoke before she left the house, but today, she didn't even think about it. She ordered her coffee, and pulled into work. As she made her way to the front door of her job, she pulled the cigarette case out, and threw it in the garbage can. She just stared at the garbage, she couldn't believe it. She had been smoking non-stop since Anthony's death, and now she was done. She turned around to face the door and looked up to the sky. "Thank you, Jesus!"

That week, Renee went to the Christian book store. She bought a new bible for her. It was a women's bible that had daily devotions in it. She bought her son a bible, and a children Christian book. She came home daily, and read her bible. She started studying the words, verses, everything.

It felt like her whole world was changing. She was talking to Anthony more at home now. She would still go to the cemetery, but found it comforting talking to him at home. Sometimes when she was in her living room watching TV with Jr., she would feel someone touching her toes. When she looked down nothing was there. This happened often, after a while she realized it was probably Anthony, then she would smile. Even her father said he was having the same thing happen when he would be sitting alone. For some reason, Anthony had a thing for trying to tickle your toes when he was alive. Now, he was doing it in the afterlife.

She also started seeing flashes of what appeared to be stars flicker when she watched TV. It was just one star that flickered. At first, she thought there was something wrong with her eyes. But then, it would happen again and again. She felt it was Anthony's spirit, and she felt comfort every time she saw it. She started going to the church she attended as a child. She rededicated her life to God, and was in a new light.

Renee had been angry at God all this time, but just like a flash of light, all that had changed. Renee was devoted. She attended bible study weekly and was reading her bible daily, getting to know Jesus. She also had private bible study classes with members at her church, at her home, and vice versa.

Now don't get it wrong, she was human. She still had her times of going in and out of depression when she thought of her baby, but then she would pray. She knew that God was a healer now, he could help with her pain of losing her son. She would always think of him, and have those days where she was down. That was her baby, he was always going to be a part of her life. Her focus now was her, Jr., and making sure they get to heaven to be with Anthony when that time comes.

In the coming weeks, two of Renee's friends lost their baby's too. Renee was there for both. No one else could relate to them like she could. They might not have lost their baby's as she did, but they all still suffered a loss.

Renee, felt she was called upon by God to help them. She was the one in town that had recently experienced the same incident that two of friends were going through. She could say "I know how you feel" because she did. Not because she wanted to make them feel better. That's what some people didn't understand.

You should never tell anyone you know how they feel after they have lost a child, if you have never lost one. Reason being, you don't know how they feel, and you never will unless it happens to you. It was good for Renee to talk to them, someone finally understood how she felt. She could tell someone how God had recently changed her mind and outset about everything.

Renee was living a new life, and she didn't need a man for nothing. Yes, she wanted companionship, but this was her time. She needed this healing time with God and Jr., something she never had before. Her focus had changed. She wanted to pursue her future in nursing school. She wanted to become a nurse ever since she was in elementary school. There was nothing she thought that she could not do.

It was now a little over a year since Anthony's death. She still visited the grave weekly, and spoke to him nightly. But through prayer and God, it was getting easier. She was still calling the detective with no return call from him. She wanted Paul prosecuted for the death of her son, but from what she knew, now, they still had not found him. How is that possible? They had his address. She just did not understand what was going on. She could never get an answer. It was making her stress at times.

Until he was arrested, and paid for what he did, this will never be over. Through prayer, Renee had forgiven Paul already. She had learned through scripture and bible study for her to move on, she had to forgive him. It was hard, how do you forgive someone who took your baby's life, the life of an innocent child of God.

Dear Diary,

I have forgiven Paul for what he has done to Anthony. I know the only way I can heal, is to forgive him. I will never, ever, ever forget what he has taken away from me! Anthony never got the chance to live his life. I will never see his first steps, first day of school, Graduation from college. I was robbed of all that at the hands of Paul! I know now, Paul has to answer to you on Judgement Day. Until, then I want him to remember every day, what he has taken away from me.

Matthew; 6:15 ERV
But if you don't forgive others, then your Father in heaven will not forgive the wrongs you do.

That immediately brought her back to her childhood. She remembered the preacher saying that in church. Now she understood what it meant. Renee blamed God for so long, when she read Matthew for the first time. That changed everything. She knew she had to ask God's forgiveness for blaming him too.

This process was truly hard on her. She spent many nights praying, fasting, and begging God to forgive her for blaming him. God spoke to her, and told her he had forgiven her from the time the words blurted out her mouth. If he could forgive her, then she could forgive Paul.

Renee had found a new place not far from where she was now. It was a three- bedroom town house with a yard that Jr. could play in. Rent was about the same, and she could still be close to her parents. Her relationship with her family had become even closer. The death of Anthony brought everyone closer.

She was surrounded by the love of her parents, family and friends from high school, and new friends. Renee had just moved, and was getting settled when she met Mike for the first time. Renee was out grocery shopping one day, when a man she noticed out the corner of her eye was staring at her. She turned around and said "Hello."

"Hi, my name is Mike. What's yours?"

"My name is Renee, how are you?

"I'm good. I was just admiring how beautiful you are." He said. "Why thank you, you're not bad yourself." He wasn't. He was about 6'2, coco skinned, had muscles for days, and a nice smile. Renee had no clue who he was. So many new people had moved into Gettysburg she couldn't keep track. On top of that, she never really went anywhere just work, school, church, and home.

"Could I have your number?" Mike asked. "Uhmm."

"I am sorry, do you have a boyfriend?" he said. "Only God!" Renee said. "That's what I'm talking about!" he then smiled. Renee gave him her number and continued shopping.

What did she have to lose, she wasn't looking for a boyfriend. It would be nice to talk to someone she thought. Renee and Mike talked almost nightly on the phone. They went out to dinner, and slowly started to form a relationship. They even started going to church together. Mike was a construction worker, he had his own car. He had been in jail most of his life. He was married before, but divorced now. His reputation around town wasn't too good. He was known for beating women, but Renee never saw that side. He was so loving towards her. They talked about their past, and what they wanted for their future. People thought because they were dating, she was having sex with him. But really, they weren't. He respected her decision not to, and that was that. She saw flaws in Mike that she thought she could change. He believed in God when they met, but was learning more with Renee.

She taught him how to carry himself in public. He had been in jail for a long time, and didn't understand a lot. She felt that she could mold him into the man she thought he could be.

In the beginning, Mike was seeing other women. Renee caught him having dinner with another woman. He said she was just a friend, but deep-down Renee knew better. After that incident, they separated briefly, then Mike smooth talked his way back in. They had been going strong, and steady for almost six months when Mike popped the question.

"Yes!" said Renee. The ring was enormous. Renee was so excited and so was Jr. He loved Mike. Mike had no kids, and he would take Jr. with him everywhere he went. Renee parents seemed pleased with Mike too. Raymond had some reservations, but he kept them to himself. He wanted to see where this was going to go.

Mike moved into Renee's place with her and Jr. It was in Renee's name. Even though they were engaged to be married, Renee always remembered what Sherry had told her. She never had a home in any man's name, only hers, and she wasn't going to stay with a man just because he was her kids father. Renee knew when they moved in together, it wasn't how the bible said to do it, but they were going to be married. She held strong to that, and stayed in her faith.

One day when Renee was home, her sister Taylor was visiting, and they were looking at TV when the phone rang.

"Hey, Renee this is Carlos, Paul's brother. Did you know that they arrested my brother, and is charging him with first degree murder of your son?"

Renee dropped the phone, her thoughts immediately went back to November 12, the day of Anthony's death.

"Renee what's wrong!" Taylor screamed. Renee couldn't talk, she just pointed to the phone. She could hear Paul's brother yelling at Taylor over the phone.

"My sister did not know he was arrested, and you should not be calling her. This is very upsetting!" Taylor slammed the phone on the hook.

Renee had been waiting for this moment for over a year now, and it had finally come. Taylor hugged Renee, and helped her pull herself back together. The time has finally come, Renee was going to have all her answers about Anthony's death finally answered in court. Through her connection with God now, Renee had peace, or so she thought. She had forgiven Paul in praying for Anthony's death, that was the only way she was going to have peace. When she would pray to God about it, he kept instilling in her she needed to do this to move on. She had, she had forgiven the man who had taken her baby's life. She was never going to forget it but, she could forgive, and she wanted justice.

Weeks later court was scheduled, and she was finally going to come face to face with him. It was the arraignment in which he was going to make his plea. Renee had brought along her parents for support, and of course Mike was with her.

"Ms. Renee Jackson?" said the DA. "Yes, I am Renee!"

"Hi, I am DA Maxwell, I will be speaking for the state. I have read through the case, I am so very, very sorry for your loss. This was such a brutal death, I am so sorry." 3Renee was completely caught off guard, what did she mean brutal death? What happened to my baby that they haven't told me? She remembered reading blunt force trauma, but something else had to happen.

"Thank you, but what do you mean by…."

"All parties please rise!" said the bailiff.

As they opened the doors, the judge walked through. Then a couple minutes later, they brought Paul in with shackles. Renee's heart dropped. He still looked the same. She wanted him to look her in the eye, but he wouldn't look her way. All the anger started building up in her again from that day. This was a man who was like a father to her kids. The judge started talking in terms that Renee had no clue. The entire process was a blur. Renee had brought a letter with her she had written months before, she sealed it and never reopened it.

She had written it right before she had got the death certificate.

"Your honor, this was such a brutal death.

This baby died of multiple blunt force drama, including broken ribs." The DA continued to talk. Renee started to fade away back to the day of the death. She started hearing mumbling. ***"Including broken ribs!" she said to herself.***

"My client pleads no contest, he does not want to put the family through a trial," said Paul's lawyer. "What does that mean?" Renee whispered to Mike. He had been through the system, he understood court language. "In laymen terms, he is basically pleading guilty Renee," said Mike.

Renee froze, the next moment she remembers is the DA asking her to read the letter. Renee slowly opened the letter, and started reading.

"My baby is gone, I will never get to see him walk, go to school. I don't know what happened or what he did," Renee stopped. This letter was not her true feelings. She didn't know all the details before she had written it. This letter was making it seemed that she still was confused. She wasn't now, she knew he had hurt her baby, and Renee broke down. The DA took the letter, and Mike helped Renee sit back down. She couldn't talk, she couldn't do anything but just cry.

He doesn't want to put the family through a trial There were more details to Anthony's death that Renee did not know, and she wanted the entire truth. Or did she? She wanted to know, but just hearing the ribs statement, she knew if she heard more she would go back to that place she didn't want to be a year ago. Everyone was saying what a brutal death, all kinds of thoughts where running through her head. The main one being, she didn't protect her son from this man.

The judge dropped first degree murder, and Paul was convicted of child abuse with a 20-year sentence. That was reduced to 5-15 years in the jail, and then five years' probation. Renee was enraged. This man took her baby's life, and would be out in five years to live as he wants. She was done, there was nothing else to be said or done. The entire ride home was long and quiet. She went to Anthony's grave, and explained to him what had happened.

"Anthony, I am so sorry for leaving you that day, please forgive mommy. I love you so much, you will always be in my heart and thoughts. You are free now baby, spread your wings and fly. Tell your great- grandparents I said hi, and your other brother/sister before you."

Renee sat beside his grave, picking the weeds along the headstone. She was letting Anthony go. She knew he would still be with her in spirit, but now he was free to fly.

Chapter 14
TRYING TO BE NORMAL

Renee and Mike were doing well. They were praying together, and going to church weekly as a family. Renee had just started a new position at a local convalescent home for nuns. She was so excited. Besides building her relationship with God, she was going to be caring for nuns. She worked hard, and she made friends quickly, but she never let them into her personal life.

Renee had been working at the home for about a month when she started building a close relationship with a nun named Sister Lucille. St. Lucille was in her late 80's. She walked slightly humped over, and always had a smile on her face. Her and Renee became close quickly. So close, that Renee felt close enough to talk to her about Anthony. Sister Lucille always told her, *you will see him again baby.* Sister Lucille taught Renee how to crochet, and Renee loved it. It took her mind off things when she started to get down. A couple months after Renee started working there, Sister Lucille fell ill. Renee was by her side holding her hand, whenever she could at work. Then one day while at home, a coworker informed her of her passing. As much as Renee wanted to go to her funeral she couldn't.

Since Anthony's death, Renee could not face another funeral, it brought back to many memories. Sister Lucille had no family around. The staff was responsible for her belongings. While cleaning her room, the manager asked Renee, "Do you want her crochet yarn and needle?"

"Yes, I will take it!" said Renee.

"Renee, look, I know we don't allow staff to have anything from the Sisters, but with you two being as close as you were, take something. A piece of clothing, something other than the yarn." said her manager.

Renee looked around, she didn't see anything at first, then she spotted a picture of Sister Lucille. She was sitting in her favorite chair as she did every day. Beside the picture was a small frame. There was something written in the frame, it read.

"Faith, Hope, Love, But the greatest of these is Love": I Corinthians 13:13

Renee reached for the small picture frame, and the picture of Sister Lucille.

"May I have these two?" Her manager nodded, and then they both hugged.

Renee went to go put the items in her locker. On her way back to her work station, she stopped at the chapel, they were having prayer.

Even though Renee was not Catholic, she respected their religion. She sat in the back, and prayed for Sister Lucille, knowing that she had finally met Anthony. As she was walking out, another Sister named Sister Elizabeth stopped her. She was a working Sister that still was out doing missions. She stayed in the west wing, with the other Sisters that were able to still live on their own.

"Hello, Renee, I want you to have this," she said. It was a hand carved statue of the Mother Mary, cradling Jesus as a baby. It was beautiful.

"Oh, this is beautiful. Why do you want to give it to me?" said Renee.

"I really don't know," they both laughed. "God told me to give it to, and that's what I am doing," she said. Renee gave her a hug, and thanked her and went back to her work station.

That next week Renee found out she was pregnant. Mike was excited, Renee was confused. She knew they were not using condoms at the time, but she took her pills faithfully. It's not that she didn't want more kids, just not now. She wanted to be married. Her and Mike had finally started having sex, but a baby was not in the plans.

"Why aren't you happy?" said Mike. "I just wanted it to be right, like with us married already you know?" said Renee. "We are going to be married Renee, we just have to re-organize some things now." said Mike.

Renee knew he was right, she was happy deep down. She knew Mike had no kids, and this was going to be his first. She called her doctor, he didn't want to see her till she was eight weeks. Per her last period, she was just around five to six weeks. So, she set up an appointment in a couple weeks for an exam.

They told people immediately, Jr. was excited he was going to be a big brother again. Renee was still attending college, but taking pre-classes for nursing. It was going to be a long road ahead. She was not going to back down. She was going to be a nurse, a wife, and have a new baby.

"Renee, I'm going to have you down at station two today," said Renee's manager. Renee didn't like station two. It was more of the sisters who needed a lot of assistance. Most of them couldn't feed themselves or assist in anyway. Renee didn't like seeing people like that, but she had to if she was going to be in the medical field.

Renee and her co-workers were all at a large table, feeding some of the sisters. It was breakfast time. They all sat together in one big area. Renee was feeding one of the Sisters when a Sister across the table started talking to her.

"What did she say?" said another co-worker. "Renee, she's pointing at you," said the co- worker that was feeding her.

Renee turned around, the Sister repeated it again, but no one knew what she was saying. The Sister's name was Sister Geraldine. She never talked, she shook her head yes and no and would look, but that's it.

"Hey, Barb, come over here and see what she is trying to say," said another co-worker.

"Say it again Sister Geraldine!" Barb said loudly.

Then as clear as day, Sister Geraldine looked directly at Renee with tears running down her face and said, "I'm sorry for what happened to your baby boy."

Tears immediately started running down Renee's face.

"Thank you. I am sorry, I need to excuse myself." Renee stood up, and walked out into the hall to the closest bathroom. No one in that entire building knew about Anthony, except for Sister Lucille, and she was gone. Renee knew Sister Lucille hadn't told anyone because she didn't leave her unit, and she didn't like half of the staff. Renee looked at herself in the mirror, "Pull yourself together, she is just expressing her concern," she said looking in the mirror. This lady had never spoken a word in years, and the one thing she says is this.

"Knock, Knock. Renee, can I come in, it's Barb." Renee opened the door. "What is going on?"

Renee proceeded to tell Barb about Anthony. Barb cried along with Renee, and gave her a hug.

"Renee, I would look at this as a message from Anthony or God." Renee didn't understand what Barb meant.

"Sister Geraldine used to have very strong visions when she was an active sister on missions. She used to heal the sick, and give messages to people from their loved ones. For her to say that to you, she could only get it from God or Anthony. No one here could have told her about your son because none of us knew." Barb looked at Renee.

Renee started thinking. She was right, it wasn't a bad thing, she said. It just really caught her by surprise. Renee put herself back together, and made her way back out to everyone. By this time breakfast was over. Sister Geraldine had been taken back to her room and put to bed. Renee decided to go to her room, she wanted to apologize for just leaving. Sister Geraldine was lying in her bed looking out the window, as she always did.

"Sister Geraldine, I am sorry for running out when you spoke. I was just so shocked to hear that, even to hear you speak. I am sorry. Thank you for saying what you did. How did you know about my son?" Sister Geraldine just continued to stare out the window.

She never said another word after that. For days after the incident, Renee went to her room. Sister Geraldine always had the same stare, and never said a word. Renee thought, if I try to talk to her, maybe she would give me a message from Anthony, but it never happened.

"Hello Dr. Drew, I keep spotting on and off. It's been like this for about three days," Renee told her doctor over the phone.

"Are you having any cramping or pain?"

"No, just little pink spotting." she said. "I don't think it's anything to worry about. Your appointment is next week, I will check you then," he said, then they hung up. Renee had had three pregnancies so far. She knew her body, this was not normal. Renee phoned Mike at work, and told him what was happening "What do you think? How do you feel?" he said.

"I don't know. I never spotted before. I'm just going to call one of my friends and go to the ER and get checked." said Renee.

"Ok, I will be there in about an hour." said Mike. He worked about 45 minutes from home. Renee headed to the hospital and phoned Debra, one of her friends to meet her there.

"Okay, let's see what's going on with this little peanut," said the nurse. She turned on the sonogram station.

"Now you are about nine to ten weeks, so you won't see a whole lot, but we should have a heartbeat." she said.

"Okay," said Renee. The nurse started to move the mouse around. Renee could see what looked like a large deformed spot. There was silence. The nurse turned around, and walked out the room. In came the ER doctor. He didn't say a word either, he picked up the mouse and moved it around. "I am sorry Ms. Jackson, but there is no heartbeat, it appears that you have had a miscarriage."

Renee turned to Debra, and started to cry. Debra, explained to the ER doctor about Anthony. The doctor put his head down, and didn't say a word.

"I am so sorry for your loss. We are going to have to do a Dilation and Curettage. We have to remove the fetus from you." He said.

By this time, Mike had walked through the door. He knew by the look on Renee's face what had happened. Mike was distraught. He wanted this baby so bad. The doctor and Debra left Renee and Mike in the room alone. After they closed the door, Mike and Renee both started crying uncontrollably. Losing a child is never easy, but they pulled themselves together and prayed.

The next day Mike took Renee to the hospital to have the D&C. It was an in and out procedure.

The sad part about it is, that they had to have Renee on the maternity unit to do it. Mike was enraged. "How come they had to do this here, where she can hear other babies crying? This is some fucked up shit!" Mike was saying to the nurse.

"Stooppp currrrssssssssing," Renee said slurring her words. That was another thing God had delivered her from, was cursing. She didn't do it anymore. She also didn't want to hear it. Renee was filled with narcotics, so she was in and out of sleep. She barely heard anything outside of Mike talking to the staff.

The procedure was over and done, and they were back home. Renee's parents had taken Jr., so it was just Mike and Renee. "How are you doing?" Renee asked Mike. "I am ok. I just really wanted us to have the baby Renee," Mike started crying. Renee held him in her arms, and began to cry. She wanted the baby too, but what could she do now? Nothing.

Renee stayed home the next couple days from work. She laid in the bed mostly, and watched TV. She started thinking of Anthony more now. She always thought of him daily, but now it was every hour. He would be three years old now, probably running around. 87In her visions, she could see him walking, and the baby she had aborted walking right beside him. Now, there was another one of her babies in heaven, watching over her now.

She didn't know if it was a boy or girl because it was too early. But, she knew her children were all together, and she wanted to be with them. Something that people don't understand with PTSD is, something can retrigger it to come back. By having this miscarriage, Renee was starting to fall into the same frame of depression as she was with Anthony's death. She didn't talk to anyone about it, not even Mike. Mike knew about her past, but she did not want to talk to him about it. Renee started to push him away, being with him romantically was the last thing on her mind. She just lost another baby. Weeks had past, Mike was trying to rekindle the magic again in the bedroom. Renee was not having it.

"Not now Mike," she said. "Well, when Renee? Ever since the baby, you don't want me to touch you." he said. "It's not that, I am just not ready. I don't want to get pregnant again right now." she said. They argued about this frequently, Mike was ready. He wanted to try again, Renee was afraid she was feeling herself go in and out of depression. She could not fathom getting pregnant again and having another loss. It was not going to happen again. She was going to make sure.

She made a doctor's appointment, and got the Depo shot without Mike knowing.

"Renee, how are you doing?" asked Barb. Everyone had heard of Renee's miscarriage at work now. "I am OK, trying to stay busy." said Renee." Have you been praying?" asked Barb. "Yes, I have." said Renee. "God has not left you now don't you leave him. You stay in his word Renee." said Barb. Renee had lied. She hadn't been praying as much as she used to since the miscarriage. She still was going to church and bible study, but she wasn't listening to God. She was just sitting in the pulpit hearing the word, but not incorporating it into her life. She didn't love God no less though.

She was slowly going back into depression. Mike was starting to become absent more and more these days, doing extra shifts. He would leave for work like three hours before it was time for him to start. Renee always thought something was off with that, but never questioned it. Renee was lying in bed one night waiting for Mike to come home from work, when she decided to pick her bible up. She turned to *Mark 9:36. And he took a child and put him in the midst of them, and taking him in his arms, he said to them, "Whoever receives one such child in my name receives me, and whoever receives me, receives not me, but him who sent me."*

She had accepted Jesus and believed he had died for her sins. What was she doing now, changing her mind because she had lost another child? Renee got on her knees, and prayed. She asked God to speak to her heart.

"Renee, I have not left you or forsaken you. I am still here as I have always been, and will be. You have to stay steadfast on my word, and what I have promised you. You have so much more to do. I am preparing you for a great walk. But, you must fall a couple times before you get there. My child, you do not understand this now, but you will. Also, some things that are in front of you are not for you. What appears good on the outside is not within. Use the gift I have given onto you, to remove those things from around you, that in the future are going to hinder you. Remember, I am in you as you are within me...."

What did that mean? She thought, what is not for me? "Mike?" Renee continued reading her bible, while still trying to figure out what God had spoken to her. Later that night, Mike returned home, Renee was asleep. He turned his phone off, stepped in the shower, and then went to bed. Renee started to see Mike in a different light after that night. Her cousin had started telling her about rumors she had heard about him cheating. Renee didn't want to believe it, she loved Mike. She felt if she would see for sure if he was, then she would handle it.

It didn't take long. Not even a week later, Mike stayed out all night. Renee phoned him several times, no response. She left message, after message, after message.

Still nothing. Then on the last call, he answered "Stop calling me!" click the phone, hung up. Renee saw red, she was so upset she called back. The phone picked up, the only thing you could hear was what sounded like a couple talking to another couple. She could hear a woman say, "Yes, we are good, he's working hard, I'm working hard." Then, she heard Mike's voice. "Well, we're getting to know each other slowly. I see her as much as I can, I work so much." Then she heard "Aww, I love you babe!" Then she heard Mike say, "Ditto." Then she heard kissing. She hung the phone up, she didn't need to hear no more. She called Debra over, and they went out back. Renee was so angry, she had borrowed a cigarette from the neighbor.

"Renee, what are you going to do?" asked Debra. "I am so upset, I poured my heart out to him. I let him in, when I really didn't want to in the beginning. Do you know how much it took for me to trust again?" said Renee.

By this time, Renee had puffed two puffs of the cigarette, and threw it down. She hadn't touched a cigarette since the night in her room when she gave her life to God. She was now upset at herself for even taking a hit of it. "I know Renee, I know, you have to be smart about this though. He is known for beating women. I know he hasn't touched you, but keep that in mind."

Renee sat down on the back porch steps, she was hurt, but she wasn't ready to confront him. She didn't know what she was going to do. Her and Debra talked throughout the night, and then Debra left to go home. Renee sat up in her room reading her bible. It was around 6:30am when she heard the back door close. Mike had entered the kitchen, he laid his keys down, and took a beer out of the fridge. As he looked up the stairs he saw the light on in the top room where he and Renee slept. He didn't know what she was going to say. He had not answered her calls, and when he did he told her not to call back. He had no idea, when he thought he had pressed ignore the last time, he really had answered the phone. That's how Renee heard the entire conversation.

"Before you start screaming, let me explain," Mike said as he stepped into the room. "There is nothing that needs to be said, you denied my calls, and told me to stop calling. Why are you here?!" she raised her voice. "I am sorry, I was confused. I have been still hurt about the baby. Every time I wanted to talk to you about the baby, you were in your own little world, always concerned about yourself. I know you hurt Renee, but what about me, my feelings?" he said.

Renee sat straight up in the bed, "Are you seriously telling me you stayed out all night, doing whatever with whoever because you were depressed about the baby! Do I have stupid written on my forehead?" she said.

"I wasn't out with no females, I was in my car just sitting. I did go out to the club with some friends, but I slept in my car because I didn't want to come back home. For what? For you to ignore me, like I'm not even here." Renee knew what Mike was saying had some truth to it. She was closed off since the miscarriage. She lost two children within two years, what did he expect. She knew she hadn't taken into consideration his feelings, because she was dealing with hers.

"I am sorry Mike! I have lost two children in two years, what do you want from me? I'm sorry I lost the baby, I am sorry I can't make that up to you!" she said crying. "BUT, that is NO excuse for you to do what you did last night!" she screamed. Mike didn't know that Renee had heard the conversation he was having with the young lady. She kept that from him that night. She was exhausted, reliving the miscarriage, and dealing with Mike's mess was too much. They made up. Renee knew if he cheated, more than likely, it was going to happen again. But, at this time, she was going to forgive him. She wasn't ready to give up on the relationship, she didn't want to be alone.

Chapter 15
WHEN A WOMAN'S FED UP

Months had gone by since the incident with Mike. Renee was still hearing rumors, but was ignoring them. She was trusting God to bring her through this. She was reading her bible even more. She had started teaching Sunday School class for the teenagers, and loved it. Renee and Jr. were at church every Sunday, just as she always been. Mike was slowly fading back from it, but was trying to claim his love for her. They still were engaged; no date was set yet. Renee supported Mike in everything he did. She was there for him when he needed her, and vice versa. He was really a good dude, and Renee brought that out even more in him. He had one major problem though, he just was not faithful. By this time, they really were not having sex, and when they were, they used protection. Renee was still on the shot. She was making double sure another baby was not going to come. Renee believed for the most part the rumors, but she wanted to catch him in the act. "Hey, you want something to eat? I am going downstairs," said Renee.

"Yeah bring me a candy bar please," said Mike.

They were having movie night in their room. Jr. was at a sleep over.

Renee had noticed that Mike was leaving his phone down stairs more often. This was so old school. She had played these games back in the day with men. Keep your phone away from your partner, and put it on silent so they can't hear it ring.

When Renee got down the stairs, she reached on top of the bookshelf and grabbed his phone. Ugh he had it locked! She played with it for about five minutes. She could not open it. She had one last try or she would lock it out. Renee closed her eyes, and ask for God's help. 85788. She keyed it in and bam! She was in. Renee was having visions like this, happening often. She would dream something, and couple days later it would happen. She knew this was her connection with God. As she listened to the messages, she heard something that dropped her to her knees.

"Hey baby, I just wanted to say hi! I love you. AHHHHHH, and the other morning was great! I still have a smile on my face. Talk to you later, I love you!" Renee knew that voice. That was the voice of the girl she heard months ago. She listened for the date, and the date was the night he stayed out all night. She fast forwarded to recent messages, and there was a woman today that had left a message. She sounded young and white. Many men in Gettysburg dated white girls, sometimes either for money or side pieces. Not all though.

Renee had some good friends who were white and dated black guys, and had a solid relationship, but there were the other ones.

"Hey Mike! You said you were going to call me, you never did. I guess you just wanted sex, and that was it. Oh well, your loss, and oh yeah, I know who your girlfriend is. You don't want her to find out about this, then you better call me back."

"Renee, damn what you doing, making the candy bar?" she heard Mike yell from the stairs. Renee quickly slammed down the phone, got the candy bar, and ran upstairs. She now had a number to call, that's what she needed.

"Hey Sarah, I need you to do me a favor," said Renee "Girl what?" said Sarah. "I'm at work, can you go by my house, and see if Mike's car is there?" said Renee. Renee worked night shift now. Some nights Jr. stayed with her parents, other nights he would stay home with Mike.

"Okay cuz I got you!" Sarah had lived in an apartment not far from Renee's, it was a quick trip. Minutes later Sarah called her back.

"Nope, his car is gone." she said.

"Thanks, cuz!" said Renee.

"What are you going to do?" said Sarah.

"I am coming home, I want to be there when he gets in." Renee got off the phone. She told her boss she was feeling ill and left work. She lived about 40 minutes from her job.

Upon her arrival home, she pulled into the drive way, and there sat Mike's car. Damn! she thought to herself, he beat me here! Renee came through the house, and nothing was out of place. She opened the basement door, and heard the dryer running. Renee opened the dryer, it was a towel and a pair of Mike's underwear in the dryer, nothing else. Renee took out the underwear, and they were damp. There was only one reason he would have this in the dryer. He had taken a hot bath and was rinsing his nasty drawls out. This is still not what Renee wanted. She wanted to catch him red handed, in the act, or coming out from the act.

Renee took a shower and headed to the bedroom. Mike was lying in the bed fake snoring. He thought he was so smart, and was dumb as a doorknob if he thought Renee was going for any of this. Renee eased in bed next to him.

"Hey baby! Why you home so early?" he said. Renee looked at him. Really, you were just snoring, but you know I am home early. She smiled, and kissed him on the forehead.

"I wanted to surprise you, I missed you!" she said. He started to go in for the kiss. Renee turned and said, "Sorry baby, don't kiss me, think I am getting sick. I don't want you to get it." He then kissed her on the head, and laid back down. Renee was not putting her lips on him, who knows where his lips have been.

She laid back and thought it won't be long now. He's going to mess up, and when he does, she will be ready. She looked up to the ceiling, and whispered to herself.

"I love you LORD, you are my strength!"

It was Friday, Mike had made plans for Renee's upcoming birthday weekend. He had reserved a room and dinner for the night. It was over $300 just for the room alone. They were set to leave tomorrow morning early. Mike was working a double, so he said.

Renee was just leaving the bank. She had moved her money to a new account. When her and Mike had first met, he didn't know how to handle money, or write checks. Renee taught him how to budget, and learn to save. They had each other's bank account numbers. Renee was setting up for the fall, she was finally ready to make a move. She had changed her accounts to different banks, she also had saved enough money to pay rent for the next six months. When Mike moved in with her, they split the bills 50/50. She was now going to be paying everything because she was kicking him out. Renee was beat, she loved Mike with all her heart.

She was sad, but ready. She knew this was not the husband that God sent for her, and it would never be. As much as she wanted to change him, she couldn't.

She was going through some clothes at home when her phone rang.

"Hello, this is Renee."

"Hello, my name is Serena. You don't know me, but I know your fiancé."

"Okay," said Renee. The young lady starting telling Renee everything she dreaded to hear, but wanted to. She was a sister of someone that Mike was cheating on her with now. Serena gave Renee dates and times of place they met. Renee knew she was telling the truth because they were all times when Renee was at work. Then Serena said something that struck a nerve.

"Also, I don't know how true it is, but he is messing with a girl that supposedly has a STD too," she said.

Renee was on fire! Her life went back to the moment she had heard she caught a STD from Paul.

Renee and Mike had stopped having sex for over a month or two now. Renee just didn't want that intimacy anymore. He tried repeatedly, she always had an excuse though. Renee had told him she was having female issues that had stopped her from wanting sex. She was going to see a doctor about it, and had just never gotten around to it. At least that's what she told him. Mike would try and try, but Renee would not budge.

He always told her that's not why he was with her, but she knew he couldn't go without it.

"Okay Serena, thank you for all you have told me, for real!" said Renee and hung up the phone. Renee went into her room and cried. She knew Mike was cheating all along, but to hear for sure and see pictures, it was finished. Serena had forwarded text and pictures to Renee's phone for proof. Renee was hurt, she had given Mike her love. It was hard to get her love. She had given it away before, and it took her baby's life. Now she has given it out again, and it has caused her heartache and misery again in a different way. Renee had all weekend to spend with this man. She was not going to confront Mike face to face with this. Mike was a big man, and strong, she really didn't know how he was going to react. Renee faked being sick, so Mike had to cancel the getaway plans they had. They stayed to in all weekend, she watched movies with Jr., and ate while Mike lifted weights and slept. Then when they were all in a room together, she conversed with him as nothing was wrong.

Monday morning had come around, Renee was up at 3:45am packing Mike's lunch as she always did. But this time she had a letter at the bottom of the lunch. Renee had stayed up that night, and written a three-page letter to Mike.

At the end, she said it was over, and when he got home she would be gone. He had till Wednesday morning to get all his stuff out of her house, and leave the key on the table. Mike had weight equipment downstairs and other large items. It was only right she give him time to remove it, but she did not want to see him.

"Hey baby, good morning!" said Mike.

"Good morning, your coffee is ready and your lunch is on the table." said Renee

"I just love you so much, I can't wait till we can take that weekend getaway," he said while hugging her from behind.

"Okay, you better get to work," said Renee. She kissed Mike on the cheek, and he grabbed his things and left. Renee watched Mike walk to the car and pull off. She then went back to sleep, she knew Mike like clockwork. He wasn't going to open that lunch box till lunch, which was at 11:30am. That would be the time her phone would ring.

Renee went to class that day, and was going to take her clothes to her parents when her phone rang; it was Mike. She let it ring, there was nothing to be said. She let it go to voicemail.

"Baby, I am so sorry! We can make this work. Please, don't let almost two years go like this. I am sorry for the wrong I have done! Please let me make it up to you! Call me, please! I love you!" Renee never returned the call.

Renee came home Wednesday, and the key was on the table. She had the locks changed that day just in case. Mike had been calling her repeatedly, but she would not answer. She had to now start the process of getting checked for any STD's. The more she thought about it, the worse she felt. Renee had set up her doctor's appointment, and started to pray, and fast.

She didn't want to have any disease. She did not want to go through this again. She started taking things out of the house that reminded her of Mike. His cologne he left behind, his shirts, even books. She wanted nothing that had to do with him in her home.

Weeks went by, and Renee had received her results, she was negative for all STD's. Renee was relieved, "Thank you God!"

Renee was still working nights at the nursing home. She had started to take on an appearance that caught the eye of one of her coworkers.

"Renee, what is going on with you?" Anna asked.

"Girl, you know I had to kick my fiancé out, it's been just stressful!" said Renee "Renee, don't let this beat you," she said. "What do you mean?" said Renee. "Girl your eyes have dark circles around. them, you have lost weight, and you're just not yourself." I know Anna! I'm just so tired with school, taking care of Jr., then getting over this break up" said Renee.

"Girl, you have to pull it together, don't let that man see you like this. He will think you are doing this over him. You need to show you are stronger and better without him!" she said. Renee understood what she meant, she hadn't seen Mike since the break-up. It was only a matter of time though.

It was a small town, everyone ran into someone daily. Renee returned home that morning. She knew in her heart this was the right decision. God had already confirmed this to her months ago, by telling her, ***Some things that are in front of you are not for you. What appears good on the outside is not within. Use the gift I have given on to you, to remove those things from around you that in the future, are going to hinder you.* "**

She knew now God was speaking of Mike. As she was about to get in the shower, she looked at herself in the mirror. She did not recognize herself. She had started to break out again. She did have circles around her eyes. She had lost weight because she wasn't eating. She would eat small bites when she ate dinner with Jr. just to make it look like she was eating. She was slipping into depression again, but this time it was showing outward. She washed her face and turned on the radio as she started to get in the shower. Donny McClurkin was belting out, "We fall down but we get up."

"I gave this man my heart, my soul, my love. What did he do, step all over it! I opened up to him, why, why, why!"

Renee began to weep and fall to her knees. She was blaming herself again for her failure she felt. God spoke to her. *"This is not your fault my child, this too shall pass!"*

She felt she had fallen, just like the song said. She was living of the world, instead of living in the world. She knew what the bible said, and wanted to obey it. She wanted to live as Jesus stated she should live. She vowed from that day, not to ever lose her spiritual connection with God.

Chapter 16

MOVING ON

Two years had passed since her break up with Mike. Renee was still going to school, and now working two jobs. She had saved and purchased two vehicles. A truck for when it was bad weather so she could get to class, and a small car to save on gas. She still lived in the same home with Jr., that was still her focus.

Her dates on Fridays nights were with Jr., watching horror movies and eating pizza. She had become more active in her church. Now she was the Youth Leader, Teen Sunday School Teacher, and had just finished her class to become the Congregational Health Nurse. She had run into Mike a couple times, and she had never looked better. He did apologize for the wrong he had done.

"Hey you look good!" said Mike. "Thanks, how are you?" said Renee. She was just leaving the local grocery store when she ran into him.

"Oh, I'm good. Hey, I really wanted to apologize for all I put you through. You are the best women I ever had, and I didn't know what I had until it was too late. You taught me a lot, and I thank you for that. I am trying to be a better man. I always think of how bad I messed up, can you forgive me?" Mike had a tear coming down his face.

"I really appreciate you apologizing, of course, I forgive you. Hey, it was a learning experience for both of us. It brought me closer to God, and now I know what I want in a husband." They talked for a little longer, and then went their separate ways. Renee had to run, she was graduating tonight!

Renee's family and friends were all at her graduation. They were so happy for her. She had gone through a lot to be on that stage, tonight she was giving the valedictorian speech. All her brothers and sisters were there, including her cousin Sarah. Her parents were smiling from ear to ear, and her son was so proud of her. She was going to be the first one of her siblings to graduate from college, it was a big achievement!

"We have laughed together, and cried together. We have been through so much to get to where we are tonight. We want to thank our teacher, Ms. Brangus, for putting up with us, and our attitudes! We would also like to thank our families for standing by us. We, as class of 2006 Nursing students, thank you all, and good night!"

Dear Diary,

It has been two years, I am happy. I am happy being alone. I needed this time alone to find out about me, and more about my God I got a chance to really reconnect with Jr., I had time to really mourn. I thought I mourned years ago, but I hadn't. I miss my baby and I always will, but I know God has brought me through this season for a reason. I have no idea what it is right now, but one day I will. I also know now that one day I will see my baby again because I am saved. I have forgiven the man who abused me when I was a child. I have forgiven the men who have hit me. I have forgiven Paul for taking Anthony's life, and I have forgiven Mike for the things he has put me through. I have not been an angel all my life, and I thank God for forgiving me for my wrongs. I know my walk will not be easy, and I am prepared for wherever God takes me.

I also thank God, for getting me through school. Now I have a career doing what I love to do. I thank you for helping me stay strong and focused, and not letting me give up. I had faith, and my faith has brought me where I am today.

Now I can say, I am ready for a husband. I want my husband to be my height, goatee, muscular, and good looking. I want him to be kind, love kids, and compassionate. I want him to be financially independent. I want him to embrace my child as his own.

I don't care if he has kids, well just one, hahahaha! Oh, and yes, he must know God, and believe in him. I know he might not be perfect, and I have learned you can't change a person. I want him to be imperfect like me, so we can continue to grow together. I want us to be as one, and to never lose sight of you!

Today....

That last entry Renee made, she drew a sketch of her future husband, and the house they would live in. A couple months later, Renee met her now husband, and lived in the same house she envisioned. The picture she also drew of her husband in her mind was identical to her husband today.

Renee has been married now for 10 years. She had three more children. She also has lost another child through miscarriage. Her husband had a daughter before them meeting, the same age as Jr. They are both currently attending college.

Renee still practices nursing, and owns her own business. She does motivational speaking in different cities. Telling her story of triumph., encouraging other women to rise above adversities.

Mother and Father - 1976

Sonya (Renee) - age 6

Sonya (Renee) and Toshia (Taylor)
1985

Sonya (Renee) - age 15

Sonya (Renee) Pregnant
with Davon (JR) - 1995

Sonya (Renee), Davon (JR) and Anthony - 2000

Davon (JR) - 2013

Sonya (Renee) and Davon (JR) - 2017

Made in the USA
San Bernardino, CA
26 January 2018